LEADING
WITHOUT
FEAR

The Fine Line between Fear and Accountability

LEADING
WITHOUT
FEAR

LAURIE K. CURE, PhD

TATE PUBLISHING
AND ENTERPRISES, LLC

Published by Tate Publishing & Enterprises, LLC
127 E. Trade Center Terrace | Mustang, Oklahoma 73064 USA
1.888.361.9473 | www.tatepublishing.com

Tate Publishing is committed to excellence in the publishing industry. The company reflects the philosophy established by the founders, based on Psalm 68:11,
"The Lord gave the word and great was the company of those who published it."

Book design copyright © 2012 by Tate Publishing, LLC. All rights reserved.
Cover design by Errol Villamante
Interior design by Caypeeline Casas

Published in the United States of America

ISBN: 978-1-62147-133-2
1. Business & Economics / Leadership
2. Business & Economics / Human Resources & Personnel Management
12.09.12

TABLE OF CONTENTS

A WELCOME NOTE

I tried.

I really wanted to do it.

I desperately sought to make it happen.

I believe that our capacity for greatness is abundant. I believe leading others is about creating inspiration and connecting to deeper human motivation. I dream of creating organizational cultures where people are truly valued and engaged; where leaders show up fully and courageously; where innovation and problem solving is effortless and people are inspired to take themselves, their teams, and the organization to a higher purpose. I have faith in the power of the human spirit when it is present and engaged, faith in its power as we immerse ourselves in "being." In these moments, we see human potential beyond increased productivity, hitting targets, and executing plans.

I want to be a part of creating cultures where there is organizational alignment of effort that drives the expansiveness of human potential. I imagine organizations where employees are working toward a shared vision. I picture organizations where individuals understand their roles and the objectives of the organization and can move into spaces that allow them to best contribute to these goals. I want to write about these dreams.

However, while I sat in a conference room, conducting focus groups with employees of a large company, I came face to face with the real issue plaguing our workplaces. Amongst thirty people, I found my heart crying out, bleeding for these individuals whom I barely knew. Some participants were angry, others crying, while others sat stoically. Regardless of where they fell on the emotional spectrum, they were all in pain. Untrusting, unbelieving, and unknowing, they were unsure how this occurred and what to do next. They felt threatened by their leaders. They were scared of losing their jobs in an economy and community where jobs were scarce. They were paralyzed in their own silence. I wish I could do justice in my description of their anguish. They sat in fear. They cried from fear. They were pained by fear.

On another day, I was with a healthy team of fifty-six organizational leaders. It was a tremendous group of powerful, capable people who had come together to continue to build their strategy for success. Seeming so opposite of the experience above, these individuals were joyous, trusting, and exemplified a true team.

As an icebreaker activity, I asked them, "What gets in your way?" I provided no further definition. The room was quiet as everyone contemplated their answer.

The response was unanimous. Fear.

"I'm afraid I don't know enough to do a good job."

"I'm afraid of failure."

"I'm afraid I won't have the resources I need to be successful."

"I'm afraid I will disappoint my team."

As I welcome you to this book and its contents, it seems that fear comes in many shapes and sizes. This is the first truth I have discovered about fear in our work. While a large percentage of the individuals I consult with discuss aspects of fear that are wounding and paralyzing, others have experienced fear in ways that ultimately supported their growth. Some people become paralyzed by fear, and others are seemingly strengthened by it. Yet it is almost certain that at some point in our lives (perhaps at many points in our lives) we have experienced fear from both these extremes. We can think of times when we were deathly afraid of losing our jobs and incomes and times when fear may have prevented us from seeking opportunities that we desired. I trust that you can also think of times when you persevered and conquered fear in a way that propelled you to something better.

This brings me to a second truth that I have come to discover about fear. I found that it often requires us to bring out a strength and perseverance that we seldom access. I have learned that prior to connecting to our individual gifts, we must also heal. We are hurting so deeply we sometimes don't even recognize the abuse we have suffered. As a consultant and a professional in psychology, not a day goes by where I don't see the impact of fear in people lives. I listen to teams share their stories, I hear leaders express their concerns, and I feel the hurt they have experienced. I also have the privilege of seeing their power and determination as they conquer these situations.

I realized something on the first day of school. It was a steaming hot August afternoon; campus was buzzing with anxious but excited students and faculty connecting with old friends, trying to find classrooms. I teach a master's level leadership and team development class at a large metropolitan university, and that night, I asked my students to consider the best leader they had ever worked for in their career. As I watched them search for that face in their minds, I was intrigued by the words they used to describe these individuals: visionary, supportive, and inspirational. The best leaders had left their mark deep in the hearts of these students. They had touched them in a profound way.

My next question: think of a second great leader in your career. Once again, their eyes rolled into their heads as they thoughtfully contemplated the question. They thought and thought. Some came up with a second. Many could not. As a whole, the students believed that in their career, only about 10 percent of their leaders were good. Only 10 percent at best. Now, I felt fearful— fearful for our employees, fearful for our leaders, and fearful for our organizations.

I hope that the stories in this book provide you with a new understanding of fear. I want to offer you hope and shed light on the various ways fear surfaces for us as employees and for us as leaders. I want them to touch you and to inspire you. I want them to serve as a reminder of how we can lead ourselves and others to greatness if we just remember what it's like to be afraid and vulnerable.

I also hope the content of this book gives you tools to grow and develop as a leader. You will gain insight and learn strategies to help you lead. I want you to share your own experiences. See yourself in the stories and feel free to share with me personally your feelings of fear. This will be a time for your healing and your growth.

While I still dream about building individual capacity and releasing everyone's potential, what I now know is that we must understand and deal with our fears if we are to be our best.

I hope you will find tranquility and peace as leaders. I believe in your power and gifts to help others do the same.

My sincere gratitude,
Laurie
www.InnovativeConnectionsInc.com

INTRODUCTION

For You As an Employee and a Leader

It was a clear, sunny morning when I met with Cindy, a nursing leader at a small hospital in rural Montana. She had recently assumed the chief nursing role and with each passing day was rapidly uncovering serious issues. The most recent, and the purpose of our conversation that day, was regarding an investigation she was initiating. She had discovered a nurse on one of the units was stealing drugs from their pharmacy. This offense not only compromised her career but also put patients' lives at risk. Worse yet, many other nurses on the unit had some level of awareness that this was occurring and said nothing. With an investigation underway, law enforcement involved, and the need to terminate employees, it all felt overwhelming. As she proceeded to provide the details of how this was occurring, her eyes glassed over, and she shook her head from side to side. We stopped for a moment to explore the emotion.

"I can't believe we have done this to our patients. How can this nurse and her colleagues have allowed this happen? How did leadership overlook this and not do anything about it? How do I help my staff recover?"

It didn't take long to discover that previous leadership had instilled a deep sense of fear in the culture— so intense that everyone from line staff to middle management was paralyzed to respond, to react, and to even notice that something wasn't right. Despite the fact that these were good people, educated professionals with licenses on the line, they potentially compromised their careers, their families, their integrity, and perhaps most important, their foundational truths. They lost sight of right and wrong; they lost the ability to hear their inner voices. They lost themselves.

You might find yourself thinking, *This could never happen to my employees or me.* You might be saying, "I would never be that kind of leader, and I have certainly never been that kind of employee." I will argue that all of us, at some point in our career, have fallen prey to the devastating impact of fear. More often than not, it is unconscious—a reaction that is so primal to our being that we sometimes are not even aware it is occurring.

I would challenge you to consider a time in your own career when you were so lost and fearful that you set aside your ideals. What circumstances lead you to ignore everything you know about right and wrong? While you might read this story in horror, consider a time when you have compromised your truth, your personal integrity, or who you are out of fear. Your situation is not likely as severe as this, but I urge you to remember. As you remember, suspend judgment of yourself or others. Remember these moments with compassion and a learning heart.

As leaders, we are always moving between two worlds. We balance the responsibility, obligation, and privilege of leading others while still being led by someone else who has the same commitment to us. Are you nurtured as a leader by your manager? What is the result of this?

As you consider these questions, let me share with you a letter. When I work with organizations and teams, I often conduct various activities in order to bring forth certain outcomes. On one such occasion, I was working with a team who was recovering from the deep pain of a previous leader. As we will discuss in the book, fear is embedded in experience. Given this, the new leader was struggling to move forward despite her best efforts to build trust. As a healing exercise, I asked each person to write a short letter to one manager in their career who had caused them the most fear and hurt. Below is one such letter.

Dear Leader:

It is with pain and sorrow that I write this note. Despite your intentions, you have left me broken. I have compromised my integrity and lost myself. I have felt from day one that I have never been on an equal playing field. You made it perfectly clear that I had better know my place and not challenge you. I was so desperate in those moments. I felt as if I needed my job so badly that I allowed you to treat me the way you did. You created a hostile work environment, and my performance had never been worse. I thought I would never recover and never be the same. I thought I was worthless. Imagine my surprise when it was you who got fired. After seven years, I can finally tell you that you cannot hurt me anymore. You cannot scare me or frighten me. Finally, people at work like me, people respect me, and more importantly, I now like and respect myself again.

Sincerely,
One of many who you nearly destroyed

I read this story with tears in my eyes. As leaders, we hold a great responsibility in our hands—a task that not many are up for and that few can execute with integrity and purpose. Every day we balance the demands of business sustainability with employee engagement. Our staff looks to us for vision, direction, and support. Sometimes it's as if they are fragile and vulnerable; sometimes they are fierce and strong. What are their hopes? What are their fears?

The purpose of this book is to support you as an employee and as a leader. Your job is tough, yet it can be one of the most rewarding and satisfying experiences you will have. I seek to provide you knowledge, tools, and lessons that will help you to improve. I believe we all want to be great leaders and great people. We sometimes just don't know how. I hope this book serves as an instrument for you to be great. It will explore the causes and impacts of fear in the workplace, ultimately providing you and your employees with active strategies to diminish the prevalence of fear in your organizational culture.

For Your Organization and the Leadership within It

As organizations experience increased demands and pressures, the need to perform often leads to organizational stress. Some leaders manage this stress by deepening relationships and building trust while others will engage in behaviors that enhance a culture of fear. Fear-based behaviors are common in workplaces today, and the impact is significant. Cultures of fear have a devastating impact on employee motivation, human performance, and ultimately business outcomes. Bottom line—leaders are seeking accountability from themselves, employees, and stakeholders in an effort to advance organizational results. However, in an attempt to reach the goal of accountability, leaders often engage in behaviors that generate fear and diminish trust.

At the core, fear is caused by a perception of threat[1]. Within the workplace, these threats are generated from a variety of sources, including threats to security, self-esteem, and belonging. The challenge for leadership becomes how to balance the need to achieve accountability with the desire to minimize fear. This book will present the causes of fear in the workplace with specific behaviors and situations that accelerate fear. Using actual stories and personal experiences as a foundation, fear will be analyzed in support of achieving the goal of accountable, trusting workplaces. The situations that trigger fear are diverse and complex, and the stories shared will reflect these dynamics, as well as allow for a personal connection and deeper meaning. In addition, effective strategies to diminish fear and enhance accountability will be provided to support leaders in managing fear within their teams and organizations.

Due to the intricate nature of emotions and how emotions function in the workplace, it is impossible to assume that we can eliminate fear and fear-based responses to the challenges we experience. What is important to recognize is that fear acts as a critical signal. Throughout the book, I will share strategies to mitigate fear. While I believe the impact of fear in the workplace has negative consequences, it is also an important reality that exists for executives, leaders, and employees. Fear is a primal, basic emotion. In today's business world, competition, economic changes, and business pressures are all environmental factors that companies experience. These realities exist, and as a result, leaders must react to them. Fear must serve as a signal or guidepost, not a way of being as we operate in organizational life. A critical point: it's not the fact that we experience fear that is the problem but rather what we do with that fear that shapes a healthy organization and differentiates success from failure. Ultimately, the success of leaders and the organization is grounded in motivating employees through emotions. In considering the relevance of emotional expression in the workplace, these experiences link to employee engagement, motivation, learning, and performance.

I hope you will use this to improve your workplace and your leadership. There are several questions and activities throughout the book. Take time to consider these questions, journal your responses, and ponder your own personal knowing.

Making the Case: Why Do We Even Care?

As we begin to explore fear, we will recognize that fear surfaces in many ways and originates from many different places. Sometimes we are fearful for our own safety and security, afraid we might lose our job. Others times we are given amazing opportunities to take on new roles or accept a promotion, and we are afraid we might fail.

Most of us will relate to all these examples. I've had personal experiences with fear—we all have. Those times when I felt like my boss had dropped me to my knees, kicked me in the face, and left me bleeding on the curb. In those moments, I felt powerless to control any aspect of my being, helpless to change my situation, and utterly defenseless. My first experiences resulted in staying in situations that were unhealthy and destructive for me personally and for those around me. As I began to better navigate fear, my response time increased. I moved between the situation and the emotion to the solution and action more rapidly. I gained skills to help guide my path through the emotion.

On the other side of the coin, I've also been a leader. Sometimes, despite my best intentions, I have used fear in an effort to get things done or meet company objectives. I have been the one who left people feeling scared and threatened. I have also been the one who provided employees opportunities to grow and supported them through their fear to great success both personally and professionally. I suspect you have been in both of these places as well.

So in my mind, it's plain and simple. We care about fear in the workplace for two basic reasons:

1. It's the right thing for our employees and us. We need to find ways that keep people whole, ways that allow them to bring their best forward. We do this not only because we want to be good leaders, but because we want to be good people. Human relationships are complicated. Actions that generate fear can seem minuscule, yet our job as leaders is to bring people's capacity into the workplace. We tap into their intrinsic motivation and watch as miraculous things start to happen.

2. It's the right thing to do for the organization. Diminishing fear will improve results. We want people engaged, productive, and healthy. We have goals and outcomes to achieve. The competitive landscapes in business are getting fiercer, and the

expectations are higher. We need effective ways to manage people, processes, and performance. Diminishing fear, and more importantly, learning more effective ways to motivate employees will improve organizational outcomes.

When we are aware of, exhibit understanding of, and navigate fear in the right way, we can achieve greatness in ourselves, our employees, and our organizations.

THE ORGANIZATIONAL GOAL:
ACCOUNTABILITY

Meet Cynthia:

> I am a kind person. I want what is best for my people. I know their family stories. I care about them as individuals, and I believe in them. I try to offer them support and guidance, but I am also held to standards. I have to achieve objectives, and my job is on the line if I do not meet our team's goals. I don't mean to lead through fear, but I know I do. I know emotions drive behavior, behavior drives action, and action drives results. Somehow I can't seem to get the top part right. My employees can be so angry and hostile. I guess they are scared too. I want to be a better leader, but I struggle to know whether they need to be fired for poor performance or if I just need to lead and support them differently. I don't know what to do. I can't tell which direction to go, and I can't get them to move.
>
> We have actions that should be steering our results in the right direction, but they're not. We have put procedures in practice to guide

employee behavior, but it's not having the impact I desire. I haven't been able to find any other way, so I have started to use threats. They seem like idol threats to me now. I tell people to do this or else. I tell them we'll all get fired if we don't meet these goals. Sometimes, I have to let someone go, and that starts a giant frenzy.

All I really want is for people to be accountable. I need them to follow through on their work, do what they need to, and get their jobs done. I just need them to do what they are told and stop arguing and fighting about everything. All they seem to do, however, is make excuses and blame everyone but themselves. They buck the process and won't get with the program.

What We Really Want Is Accountability

When we think about emotions, and specifically fear, in the workplace, it is important to remember what the organization ultimately wants to accomplish. At the end of the day, the business needs to successfully meet its strategic objectives, whether those are financial, customer satisfaction, employee satisfaction, or operational goals. One of the major impediments to achieving organizational goals is the lack of accountability by leaders and employees within the company. It becomes an intricate web as we seek to understand the relationships between accountability, trust, conflict, communication, and emotions, especially fear. What we know, however, is that there is a fine line between holding individuals accountable and increasing the level of fear in the organization. What we also know is that when fear prevails, outcomes and results suffer.

Therefore, what we seek as leaders and employees is the ability to find passion in our work and present ourselves in a way that meets our personal needs and the needs of the organization. When we can better recognize the prevalence and usage of fear in our organizations, we can implement leadership strategies to decrease it and thereby improve results. It all sounds simple, doesn't it? It actually can be if you allow yourself the ability to release your own fears and do what's right for people in your organization. Let me repeat the first part of that statement—it is a very important point. You must release your own fears.

As a leader, you are held accountable for your behaviors, actions, and results. As a leader, you hold others accountable for the same. What we often fail to recognize, however, is the beginning of this chain starts with emotions. If we can begin by managing our emotions more productively, then behaviors, actions, and results fall into place. It's the driver to achieve our desired results.

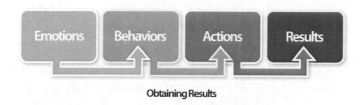

Obtaining Results

The Process of Accountability

Accountability is about establishing clear expectations, seeking mutual commitment from employees around those expectations, and holding people responsible for the commitments they make. It's about moving employees (and ourselves) from victim behaviors such as blaming, denial, and confusion to actions that demonstrate ownership—ownership of our choices, our efforts, and our work. Trust, relationships, communication, conflict, and other leadership skills can help us achieve accountability, but fear will largely undermine all those efforts.

Establishing Accountability

Establish Clear Expectations

Leaders use fear at all stages of this continuum. Often we begin by not creating clear expectations, and as we will learn in subsequent chapters, this uncertainty of what is expected elevates the fear response for both the employees who report to us and ourselves. In establishing clear expectations, we need to create a common understanding and be certain of the outcome desired. We need to deliver a clear vision and, when possible, define actions to achieve that vision. There are times when you as a leader might not have the clarity that you need to provide direction to others. In these cases, gaining the necessary information to provide a direct vision is critical. Others cannot be held accountable for expected behaviors, actions, and results without clear expectations of what you desire. The more you can create safe, open discussion around expectations, the more commitment you will receive at the next stage of the process.

In establishing clear expectations, ask yourself:

- Have I established clear expectations for this project or situation?
- Do I need more information in order to communicate to my employees?
- Have I allowed for open, honest communication about the expectations and necessary next steps?
- Have I allowed my employees to be involved in this conversation?
- Did my employees or team ask questions that would lead me to believe they understood the expectations?
- Would my employees feel safe to say that the expectations were clear or not clear to them?
- If I asked my employees if they knew what was expected of them, could they tell me with accuracy?

Fear results from a perceived threat that is enhanced by the unknown[2]. The more you can reduce the uncertainty, the less fear you will see in your workplace.

You can do this as a leader or an employee. We can all take responsibility for getting more clarity on expectations.

Seek Mutual Commitments

The next phase of accountability requires that we gain commitment. When we use fear to gain commitment, we are lying to ourselves, and others are lying to us. We get a false promise, backed by an inaccurate assumption of a perceived commitment. Commitment is about mutual agreement. Fear might (and I say *might*) lead to compliance, but it never leads to a true commitment. When we use fear at this stage, we get employees who move into paralysis and begin operating under the "just tell me what to do" principle. This is neither effective nor helpful. It creates an environment where people collapse into themselves as they seek to do what they are told. Creativity suffers, innovation falters, and productivity moves at a standstill.

In gaining commitment, ask yourself:

- Have I provided a forum for open, honest discussion about the commitment and any concerns or questions my employee(s) might have? If your employees are silent, you are likely not creating a safe space. People might be in a place of fear and scared to speak up.
- Have I allowed my staff the opportunity to actively participate in discussing the problem, creating solutions, and defining expectations? The more involved people are in the process,

the more likely they will be committed to the outcome.

- Can my employees articulate the reasons we are doing what we are doing? If they cannot, it will be difficult for them to commit. They will not see the reason or importance and therefore not engage successfully.
- Have I gained mutual commitment from my staff? Do I have buy-in regarding this issue? How do I know I have this commitment? Just because people nod their heads does not mean you have commitment. Be sure they are on board. You will only know this through safe and open communication. Pay attention to the non-verbal signals they might be sending, as well as what is spoken. Non-verbal signals might include silence, heads bowed, or minimal eye contact.

Remember, commitment and compliance are different concepts. Sometimes compliance is enough, but most of the time you will be more successful ensuring you have gained the level of commitment you need.

Hold People Responsible for Commitments

Leaders will often use fear in the last phase where they are seeking to hold people responsible for the commitments they have made. Accountability does not require punishment. The word *consequence* does not have to equate to reprimand. When we actively hold people responsible, we must engage in difficult conversations. It requires that we have laid the foundation from the first two steps of the process. Leaders, however, will often take a punitive approach to these discussions for several reasons.

First, we often resort to fear because we don't have the skills, ability, or sometimes the courage to effectively manage the first two steps of the process. If we have effectively set expectations and gained buy-in and commitment, the final stage becomes simple. If we have not, then holding people accountable to the outcome gets very sticky. We are suddenly in a place where we must "deal with" employees who didn't perform to our expectations. If we consider this dilemma from the perspective of emotion, it's possible that we actually find ourselves resorting to threats and punishment as a way of deferring blame from ourselves onto others. At some level, we might recognize that perhaps we are at fault from the beginning by not leading as effectively as we desired. If that is the case, we project our fear of inadequacy onto our employees, leaving them to hold the blame.

There are times when managing employees through a disciplinary process is the necessary and the correct course of action. However, I will argue that this should not be the norm, nor does it have to be a process that induces systematic levels of fear throughout your team or organization. When you arrive at this step of the process, be sure you have adequately managed the first two stages effectively as a leader. Ask yourself whether you sufficiently established clear expectations. Have you gained the commitment you need to achieve results? If you can honestly answer no to these questions, it is important to reestablish the agreement and start over, giving your employees the opportunity to perform. If your honest answer is yes, then your course of action might need to take the path of a crucial conversation. Having this difficult discussion while continuing to minimize fear is a challenge that we will explore as we proceed. It is possible, however, to hold this conversation in a way that limits fear for the employee and the rest of the team.

We might also use fear because we are being led by leaders who are using this approach. Our natural tendency is to mimic behavior. We have done it since we were children, modeling our teachers and parents. It takes a great deal of conscious awareness, particularly in organizational cultures of fear, to use a different approach. In cultures of fear, we all shut down and lose our ability to be creative. Unfortunately, that includes creativity around addressing fear. Ask yourself whether your leader is fear based. If so, how do you need to lead differently? How do you engage in different conversations from a place of awareness?

Along these same lines, if we haven't communicated effectively throughout the entire process, fear can be the resulting response. As we will discuss in subsequent chapters, leaders communicate and deliver messages all the time. We deliver messages that we don't agree with, we communicate realities that are not pleasant, and we must somehow continue to navigate this thing called *accountability*.

Sometimes when I work with leaders, I hear, "It's not my responsibility to manage the emotions of my people. I have a job to do, and if that scares them or makes them angry, I have no control over that."

I believe our responsibility as leaders is to treat people fairly and achieve organizational results. We can do this concurrently. The hope is these two items follow one another. We can lead in ways that minimize negative emotions, knowing that when we lead from fear, we are less likely to achieve our goals. We aren't as productive, our employees don't create new and better solutions to problems, and absenteeism and turnover increase. These outcomes are viewed as the responsibility of the leader, and while you will never eliminate all negative emotions (nor would you want to), you can lead from a place that minimizes the negative impact of these emotions.

Finally, we use fear because we don't know any other way. I hope throughout this book you will learn that using fear is not an ideal way to manage and there are better solutions to get the results you desire. There are times when employees will experience severe consequences for their actions. I am not suggesting that you cannot or should never terminate an employee or write someone up. What I am suggesting is that these actions should not be delivered from a place of threat but rather a place of natural consequences to inaction or inappropriate action. If we understand fear, we can lead in a way that reduces it, thereby enhancing trust and communication. The line between fear and accountability is fine. As we seek to achieve accountable workplaces, we will often cross over the line, using fear as a mechanism for accountability. What is important is readjusting our course when we recognize we have crossed over the line and redirect our actions such that fear is reduced.

THE LANDSCAPE OF EMOTION:
HOW EMOTIONS SHAPE OUR WORK LIFE

Meet Tom:

I have worked with Tom for over a year now. He is a humorous CEO who takes pride in his logical, critical thinking. Every time we meet, I ask him, "How do you feel today?"

He responds, with a smile and wink, "I think I am feeling good."

This banter offers a nice way for us to begin to engage in our executive coaching work together. Our joke comes from an understanding and appreciation of our differing personality styles. He considers his decision making to be highly analytical. He reviews scenarios, spreadsheets, and data. He crunches the numbers and compiles information. However, after working with him, I am beginning to see the truth of how this really works. What I see in him is a leader with a fierce gut instinct. He is a leader with an internal knowledge of what to do and exactly how to do it. As we consider Tom, he offers a nice example of how logic and rational intersect with emotions and feeling as we navigate decision making in the world.

The Importance of Emotions

We cannot talk about the emotion of fear without first understanding the premise of emotions in general. As humans, we are emotional beings. Emotions shape our lives in ways that reflect who we are and what is important to us. While we often want to believe that our rational, logical side is governing our decision making, particularly in the work setting, it is actually our emotional nature that allows us to function. Sometimes we seek to hide this part of us, believing that it has no place in the business world. Other times, we actually tap into this deep sense and feel our way through situations. More often than not, we are blending and merging the best of both these worlds to create a healthy balance and stimulate the best course of action in any given circumstance.

As we consider the idea of emotions, there is a continued recognition that, since the age of Aristotle, there has been a constant struggle between head and heart with an inadequate appreciation of the intimate relationship between the two perceived extremes. In organizational environments, rationality tends to be pervasive, and the demonstration of emotional expression, either positive or negative, is dismissed. Often, leaders make the inaccurate assumption that one can manage and lead without taking emotional aspects into consideration. This is a dangerous notion given that all our reactions and responses are driven from an assessment of our emotional condition, whether we are willing to admit it or not. What we need to recognize is emotions and cognitive thinking do not exist at opposite ends of the continuum. In reality, we integrate thoughts and feelings seamlessly and use both as we assimilate our experiences and make all our decisions.

While this is not designed to be a theoretical discussion of emotions and their psychological origin, it is important to provide a foundational understanding of emotions and how they surface. Emotions surface when a given event interrupts our normal cognitive state[3]. Additionally, they are impacted by the meaning we associate with various situations we encounter. As a result, emotional experience begins with an event but is influenced by numerous other variables including aspects of affect, mood, personality, cognition, motivation, and values[4].

At the core, emotions are reactions to events or circumstances that occur in our lives. Emotions saturate our work life. We feel joy and pride, stress and burnout, anger and fear. Our emotions reflect the intense demands placed on us and our ability to individually and collectively balance these demands. They reflect what is important to us and offer wisdom that guides us. Within organizations, human capacity and the efforts of employees drive results and performance. Emotions serve as a guidance system to aid individuals in regulating judgments, behaviors, and actions, thereby supporting goal achievement. Integrating these emotions becomes the critical task of leaders as they seek to motivate, expand capacity, and achieve outcomes from employees.

Daniel Goleman popularized the theory of emotional intelligence (EI), making the term not only mainstream but relevant in a business setting. The premise of EI is that individuals need to learn how to have awareness and govern their emotions in order to support their ultimate goal. With EI it's about how we perceive, control, and evaluate our emotions. In this way, it will be important to understand how emotions are developed, expressed, and regulated at work if we are to better manage fear[5].

What Are Emotions?

We are all different. We have different values and different personalities—all of which motivate our behavior. It is these differences that make us who we are. It is these differences that both strengthen our workplaces and also create conflict in our organizations. It is also these differences that generate variation in how we experience and express emotion.

Emotions begin with these variables—values, personality, and motivation[6]. They are activated by who we are and what is important to us as individuals. Illustration 3 demonstrates how the constructs of emotion work together. Our goals are generated, both consciously and unconsciously, by aspects of personality, values, and motivation. These items drive what we view as critical for our personal well being, and thus, we create goals around them. Our goals reflect what we want from a given situation or event. They help us to define what we seek to accomplish from our circumstances. Our goals are always impacted by assessments, appraisals, and judgments that we make about events. Those determinations and assessments occur as we decide whether a given event is supporting or hindering our goals. Our answer to these questions then produces a given emotional reaction. It occurs in an instant as an automatic reaction to the events we experience in our lives. We will begin to explore each segment individually and hopefully create a picture of how they each impact our emotional responses.[7]

Drivers of Emotion

Activity

Think about what happened to you throughout the entire course of your day. Look at the events of your day as if you were viewing them with a video camera (as a third-party observer). Consider various events from the time you woke up to the time until you returned home from work—perhaps even beyond that, until you were ready for bed. Make a list of all the emotions that you experienced during this time. How did those emotions impact your decision making?

Perhaps you were greeted with a smile and felt grateful. Maybe you attended a heated meeting and returned to your office angry. What impact do these emotional experiences have on your subsequent choices? How might your choices have been different if your emotions were different?

Consider your daily emotions as if watching them in a movie. Don't judge them or analyze them—just notice.

I tend to be a person filled with emotion. There is no denying it. As I conducted this activity the first time, my powerful learning was how easy it was for me to hold negative emotional energy. Small situations that triggered self-doubt or frustration would stick with me for hours after the event had passed. I often blew them up in my mind, making them more significant than they needed to be. As I learned from this, I came to realize that fleeting emotions didn't need to impact my overall mood. When they did, my choices from that point forward were infected and altered.

What is your critical learning as you conduct this activity? What were your insights?

_____

_____

Emotions Are Impacted by Personality, Values, and Motivation

Meet Joseph and Bill:

Joseph was the CEO of a medium-sized distribution company. As a leader with six thousand employees, he prided himself in loyalty, integrity, and always speaking the truth. His personality made him very thoughtful and deliberate in his decision making. Joseph has been around the block and understands how businesses operate. He believed a hard day's work will yield results. His division was highly successful, and he performed well. Joseph's employees liked him. They respected his style and wanted to work hard for him. Joseph was an introvert and tended to need time contemplating issues before he arrived at a solution. He was not a *cheerleader* for the team or the company. When he delivered a message, it was important to him that he communicated the most honest message he could—straight up, black and white.

Bill was a CEO for a large company as well. With five thousand employees under his leadership, he had a gift for seeing the big picture, painting a vision, and establishing relationships with his employees. At the same time, Bill always looked into every detail to ensure nothing was forgotten. He valued relationships and worked to ensure people were treated well. He worked hard, and his performance was stellar. His division was amongst the most successful in his company. He also valued fun and excitement in his life. One could say that he was a cheerleader for the division, and his people responded. They celebrated accomplishments, and he often had large events to demonstrate appreciation for staff. Bill's people loved working for him, and they always put their best foot forward.

Joseph and Bill are both great leaders. Although they have different personalities and may hold different values, they are effective and respected. Consider how these two individuals might share difficult or challenging news with their employees. What if they had to lay off employees due to budget cuts or ramp up production to meet increased targets? How might their approach be different from one another? Now, consider how Joseph and Bill might feel about these difficult situations. How might they express their emotion to others?

Due to their different personality styles and core values, both these leaders would likely manage situations in a very different way. Joseph values honesty and straight-forward communication. Bill values relationship as a core variable. While they are both excellent leaders, what is important to them and what they are motivated by will drive them to respond in their own unique way to similar situations. Given this, the way they lead, communicate, and hold others accountable will differ based on what is most important to them at the core.

Emotions Are Complex

The experience of emotion is fluid. We can attempt to isolate aspects of emotion or specific emotions, but in reality emotions are always ebbing and flowing—an ongoing process of actions and reactions, a give and take of exchanges. Our goals change effortlessly throughout situations. They fluctuate unconsciously throughout our interactions. Our judgments and appraisals are altered without notice. We can adjust these variables instantaneously as we interact with others, and we know that in any given situation we will experience a plethora of emotions. In the course of a one-hour meeting, you might find that you have feelings that span all across the continuum from positive to negative and back again[8].

Personality, beliefs, and values all contribute to our encounters with others. They impact who we are and thus impact our goals. They affect our evaluation of experiences and hence our emotion. Personality and values help us to define who we are and what we stand for.

As we consider what motivates us, it is those things that aid us in defining what is important and unimportant in our situations. Ultimately, these basic aspects of who we are drive our goals and our emotional reactions. As affect, moods, emotions, and feelings interact, each is playing a part in how individuals evaluate various situations and thus how they respond emotionally. Emotions reflect what is important to each of us personally and help gauge progress toward important goals that reflect sacred and core personal values.

If Joseph and Bill had to identify their number-one core values, they would be very different. If we considered aspects of their personality, the constructs might be very opposite. Both leaders will express emotion differently based on the fact that what is important to them varies. What we can tell through emotions, though, in all our encounters, is what is important to others and us.

I personally have defined relationships as my number-one value. There is no right or wrong value, but that is the value most important to me. Others might say responsibility, loyalty, or integrity is their number-one value. When called to make a decision, I will always lead from a place of relationships. That will guide me down a much different path sometimes than people who lead from other core values. It doesn't necessarily make decisions or approaches better or worse. There is no judgment. It just makes our emotions and choices look different since our starting place varies, and it can make our leadership challenges different.

Activity

There are many formal tests and assessments that help you understand your personality. If you have not already taken one of these assessments, consider taking one and exploring the critical aspects of your personality. If you have taken one, take a moment to reflect on what you learned. What were the key takeaways from your assessment? Tests you might consider are: Meyers

Briggs Personality Indicator, DISC, StrengthsFinder, or the Enneagram. There are often versions of these assessments that you can take on the Internet. Consider whether you are an introvert or extravert. How do you make decisions? Are you a big picture thinker or more detail oriented? Are you organized or spontaneous?

_____

_____

_____

_____

_____

Take a moment to consider your personal values. What is most important to you? Start by making an exhaustive list of all of your values. This might be twenty or fifty. Make a list of all your values and then prioritize the top five and write them here.

1. _____

2. _____

3. _____

4. _____

5. _____

Now, conduct this activity with your staff. What do each of your direct reports value? What are key aspects of their personality? How do these differences impact how you lead or how your team shows up? What are your key takeaways as you consider your team?

_____

_____

_____

_____

_____

Lesson #1: Understand Yourself

Who we are alters our emotional experience. Emotions serve a vital role in regulating our judgments, behaviors, and actions.[9] They support us in achieving our goals and provide us with guidance as to whether we are proceeding on the right path. Our personality, values, and motivation seek to help us define what is important and what goals will align to our needs. Emotions then reflect what is important to each individual personally and help gauge progress toward important goals that reflect sacred and core personal values.

Knowing what we value and how our personality surfaces will impact our emotional display. As we react with emotions, we can usually assume something has triggered our values or what is important to us. When Joseph receives a compliment from his leader about his thorough decision making and hard work, he will likely feel very appreciative and happy. This compliment aligns with his values. If Bill was told his staff didn't like and respect him, he would be devastated. That would conflict with his core values. This personal definition of what we find meaningful is the center of our experience and helps to define our goals, our appraisal, and ultimately our emotions. The main premise of emotions is the assertion that emotions are cognitive and differ by how situations are interrupted by each individual. Motivational elements of what is important and unimportant create and drive the emotional reactions that follow.

Therefore, motivation plays a key role in emotion.[10] Decision-making, judgment, and behavioral tendencies are linked to motivational desires[11]. For fear it might be the motivation to avoid harm. The harm might be along any of the elements of the motivational continuum—from security or belonging to feeling appreciated and loved. Given that goals drive motivation and motivation aligns to emotion, understanding the intricate relationship between these variables is important in application of emotion in the organizational environment. Knowing who we are and what is important to us can help to determine what motivates our happiness and joy or anger and fear. This understanding of our employees and ourselves can be critical in shaping behaviors that support movement toward positive outcomes.

Emotions Are Goal Oriented

Meet Julie:

Julie was a seasoned leader with over twenty employees who reported directly to her. She worked in the manufacturing industry, and her days were long. She was always challenged to ensure she was adequately supporting her team. They had difficult jobs that were physically demanding. They were consistently trying to make ends meet financially, and they often had struggles at home.

Like many organizations, Julie's company delivered an annual employee satisfaction and engagement survey. Julie's results had always been amongst the top 10 percent of leaders nationwide. The second year she received her scores, she discovered, once again, she had surpassed the company record and received the highest employee engagement score in the company. As she shared the results with her team, she felt happy, cheerful, and pleased. They celebrated with a team luncheon, and she gave everyone a personal note of thanks. She knew her people were among the best, and she was proud that they had felt the same way.

She had met the company goal and her professional one by achieving high engagement. She felt good that she had met the objective. Additionally, she had achieved her personal goal of ensuring the team enjoyed their work, felt supported, and remained engaged in what they did. It was important to her that the team continued to feel pride in their work.

As Julie and I explored the idea of emotions, I asked her to consider playing out the example in a different way. I asked her to imagine that the second year she received her annual engagement score and the results went down ten percentage points from the first year. As she considered this example, she recognized that she would feel disappointed, angry, and perhaps confused—unsure as to why her results suffered. Now, I asked her to consider what she would feel if she was the lowest-scoring manager in the company. What if she were at risk of being fired as a result of the low score? At this point, Julie began to feel defensive, embarrassed, and fearful.

This example seeks to demonstrate one of the foundational aspects of emotion. Our personal goals serve as the pivotal axis for what emotion we feel at any given moment in any given situation. As such, individuals experience positive emotions when an event is viewed as supporting personal goals, and a negative emotion is experienced when the event is seen as hindering or obstructing those goals. Thus, emotional reactions are generated by events that help or hinder our personal needs and objectives for our well being.

We also know if two leaders received the exact same score on their survey, they are still likely to have two different emotional reactions. For example, let's assume two leaders both score 4.0 on a five-point scale for the annual employee engagement survey. That might reflect an increase for one leader and lead to a feeling of excitement, while the other leader might have gone down from 4.3 to 4.0, thereby leaving him feeling disappointed—same event, same score, two different responses—all based on an individual goal.

You can use any number of examples to demonstrate this point. What we know, however, is various dimensions drive our emotional response. At the core of our emotional response is the goal we are seeking. Ultimately, we ask, "Does the event support me or get in the way of me achieving my goal?"

As demonstrated, emotions are goal oriented. If we consider emotion and the discussion above, it becomes evident that emotions are grounded in motivation toward the achievement of a certain goal. We are always cognitively assessing whether an event or situation will harm or benefit us and whether the event is positive or negative compared to our goal. More than other factors, the emotion we reveal and express is about the goal and our interpretation of the situation in relation to that goal. Illustration 4 demonstrates that when events support our personal goals, we will experience positive emotions. To the contrary, when an event obstructs our goals, we will feel some negative emotion. The key question becomes: what is your goal?

The Relationship of Emotions to Goals

Personal well being helps us to define our goals. Clearly, we will seek behaviors and outcomes that support our personal needs. Emotions, then, help us to regulate our behavior in ways that move us closer to our goals. If we begin to recognize that a given action or behavior is inconsistent in helping us to achieve a goal, we will respond emotionally and rationally in other ways. As a leader, if I find that working with a certain person drives me crazy, I will likely not volunteer for assignments and projects that partner me with that individual. That event (working with the certain person) leads to a negative emotion (craziness), which does not support my personal needs (stability and happiness). I will consequently learn from this experience and, in order to avoid feeling the negative emotion in the future, I will select different people to work with. This cycle of learning contributes to our ability to achieve the goal we seek.

Often we are consciously aware of our goals. In the workforce, they can be large objectives established to achieve organizational success. For example, we might have sales targets or market share projections that we must reach. Maybe we have retention goals or customer-satisfaction measures. Perhaps our goals are smaller and include making sure a project gets completed or that an employee is given time off to care for a sick child. While we might have a conscious awareness of many of our goals, most of our goals are less conscious. Often, we experience an emotion and may not be sure why. These are times when a situation is impacting a goal, but we aren't aware of what the goal is. As we talk about strategies later in this book, enhancing self-awareness is a critical first step. It is from this awareness that we can assess, regulate, and manage our emotional experience in a way that serves us and others.

Whether you feel happy or proud, frustrated or fearful, ask yourself, "What is my goal in this situation?" Perhaps you were seeking recognition for your contribution to a project, and by not receiving it you felt devalued. Maybe you wanted to feel like the expert on a certain topic, and doing so made you feel proud. Possibly you wanted fair treatment for your staff, and a given event left them feeling insulted. All of these examples demonstrate the link between goal and emotion.

Activity

Consider a personal example. Start with an emotion you have recently experienced. Perhaps you felt excitement, compassion, pride, or anger. List your recent emotion.

Emotion

_____

Now, let's work backward. What was the event that generated that emotion? What occurred to lead you to that emotional experience? What did you want or desire?

Event

_____

Continuing to work backward. As you consider the event, what was your goal in that situation? What were you hoping to accomplish?

Goal

Consider the impact if your goal had been different. How might your emotional experience have been altered? For example, if you wanted to achieve consensus for a recommendation you had and everyone disagreed with your idea, it might have left you feeling discouraged and angry. What if your goal was to get input and share ideas? What emotions would you have experienced differently? Perhaps you would have felt energized by the brainstorming or enlightened by the creativity.

This activity seeks to explore the premise that, while we think emotions are generated by events, the goal of our interaction really serves as the foundation. When we understand our goals, we can better manage our entire emotional experience.

Lesson #2: Know Your Goal

Knowing your goal is about understanding what you want to accomplish. It is also about knowing when you need to keep the goal the same or change it. Remember that our emotional experiences are signals—signs that are meant to help direct our decision-making. When we have a signal of any kind, we need to pay attention.

The question becomes: what message is the signal sending me?

A green light tells us to go. Dark clouds in the sky tell us it might rain, and generally a ring on the left hand means that person is married. Our emotions offer us the same basic wisdom. When we feel happy in a given situation, it can signal to us that we are on the right track—we should continue as directed. When we feel afraid, something is wrong, and we might need to respond differently. When we are confused, we may need to seek more information. All of these emotions serve as a guidance system to let us know if we are proceeding correctly. When we ignore the signal, we experience the consequences—destined to repeat the lesson again.

Sometimes our emotional responses tell us that we need to consider changing the goal. Other times, it might be reinforcing that our goals are on track. Remember, negative emotions are not always bad. Again, they serve as signals. They can help us better understand what we want, what is important to us, and how we might need to change in order to grow. There is no need to judge our emotions. Just be aware of them.

Goals in this context are not always the lofty organizational benchmarks that we are required to hit. They are small subsets of what it important to us. When my husband and I cook, my goal is to have fun together, try new things, and serve a healthy meal for the family. When we turn the music up, dance around the kitchen, and pull out a new recipe, my goals are met, and I have positive emotions. When he breaks out four sticks of butter and throws it into the pan, I am beginning to feel some negative emotion. The butter is a bit contrary to my healthy meal goal. So I can react from that place and get angry and stay in a negative emotional state (and now impact my husband's emotional state). I could also use another ingredient (like olive oil), which I might perceive to be healthier, thereby maintaining my original goal and now moving back to a place of positive emotion. Or perhaps I readjust my goal in order to maintain a positive emotional state. I decide I want a really a delicious meal at all costs—throw on the butter and let's have some fun.

When we begin to get clear about the goal, it can help us to understand our emotions. When we understand our emotions, we can better gauge our reactions. We are sometimes so rigid in our goals that we fail to see opportunities and other explanations. In the workplace, you might consider how often you enter a meeting or an encounter with a preset outcome. If you just shifted the smaller goals, you might create space for wonderful options to emerge.

Emotions Are Based on Our Personal Judgment of a Situation/Event

Meet Karen:

Karen had just lost her father to a four-year battle with cancer. She and her mother had been at the hospital all night and called all the family members to let them know about his passing away. They had been crying and felt exhausted both physically and emotionally. As she left the hospital with her mother, they both got into separate cars to drive home and begin making the final arrangements. They proceeded out of the parking lot with Karen following her mother. As they entered an intersection, her mother proceeded to make a left turn and pulled right in front of another car. The other driver slammed on his brakes as she continued to drive, seemingly unaware of the accident that almost transpired. The other driver was furious, honking his horn, waving his hand in the air, and screaming obscenities.

He assessed that Karen's mother was a poor driver who wasn't paying any attention. He blamed her for almost causing an accident and was angry by her inability to notice his rant. His anger continued as he drove on to his destination. What if he would have known the situation? While he might have still been frustrated by her lack of awareness behind the wheel, would he have been more tolerant, more sympathetic, or more careful? How would his emotion of anger shifted if he would have assessed the situation differently?

We make similar judgments all the time. When we see homeless individuals on the street, do we feel disgusted and frustrated, assessing that they are lazy or alcoholic? Do we feel empathy, believing that at any time that could be us? When our employees come in late to work, are we angry, assessing that they must be irresponsible? Or are we concerned because we think something must be wrong? When our team is silent in a meeting, do we assume they are all on board or that they are fearful to respond? We make these assessments all the time in conjunction with other facts and history to support our appraisal. Sometimes we are correct in our judgments; sometimes we are not. What is important to consider at this point is that we experience emotion based on our judgments of the situation—whether those assessments are right or wrong.

Emotions Are Driven from Our Assessment and Appraisal

From some of the examples above, we are beginning to see the complexities of emotion. We have likely known about these complexities all along. This might be the main reason leaders for centuries have tried to isolate emotions and remove them from the work experience. However, the challenge continues.

As presented, the first variable contributing to our emotions are the goals we are seeking. Our personal goals are key drivers of what emotion we experience, and hence, display. This can help us to understand how the same event can trigger different emotions and reactions in two different individuals (e.g., a score on a survey).

The second variable that contributes to emotion is the personal evaluation we place on the situations and events. The way we evaluate events and assign meaning to them is impacted by a number of factors. These factors include external variables, our level of control of the situation, or who we determine might be responsible for the event. We might look at how much effort is required in a given circumstance or the degree of certainty we have about a given situation. As we feel various emotions, it is a result of each of these variables changing. All of these items impact our appraisal in different ways. As our appraisal is affected, so is our emotional response. As these items change, the emotion we feel changes as well.

As we consider these elements in relation to fear, research shows that fear involves a high degree of effort and that it results from an appraisal where the individual feels little personal control of the situation. This means that when we are in fear (or those around us are in fear), it is because we feel a lack of control over aspects of our life that significantly impact us. As a result, we will expend a great deal of energy and effort trying to manage fear in order to regain power over it. In addition, with fear, we usually deem others responsible for the event, and there is a high degree of uncertainty in the outcome. This makes sense as we consider it in relation to control. If we feel helpless to control our situation, than we assess that someone else must be in control and therefore we shift responsibility.

The important item to consider at this point is that if any of these dynamics changed, then you would feel a very different emotion than fear[12]. These aspects or variables make up the ingredients for fear. Like a recipe, we know that for fear to exist, these items must be present in the environment or with the situation. One of the strategies we will discuss in relation to this concept and its alignment to fear is how individuals can get more control of the situation. Since we know fear is produced by an individual feeling they have little control over a situation, one could deduce that increasing personal control would change the level of fear experienced. This is a critical point as we consider the ability to manage emotions. If we want to shift our emotional experience, we must alter the variables that result in our assessing the experience in a given way. Essentially, we must change the ingredients.

If we look at this from a different perspective, we can see how these concepts play out with various emotions. For example, happiness is a positive emotion that occurs almost at the other end of the continuum from fear. With happiness, the individual is seen to be highly responsible for the event or condition. There is a perception of greater control by the individual and certainly a lower level of effort[13]. When we are happy, it is generally because an event supports our goal in a positive way and we believe that somehow we contributed to that event. With the significant change in the core ingredients, we came up with a completely different emotion—happiness.

As we consider this in relation to fear, the challenge surfaces when we realize that increasing accountability often results in a higher level of fear. Since achieving accountability requires that we assume ownership for situations, it seems intuitive that fear and accountability can often work at odds with one other. As we seek to drive more accountable workplaces, we must understand that we have to manage the ingredients of control, effort, certainty, and responsibility in order to decrease fear and enhance individual ownership. It is only when we navigate these variables that our outcome will change.

Let's consider a leader who is dealing with an employee who is not performing. Employee relations issues always involve a high degree of effort, and generally that effort is reflected in the leader's emotional experience. Revisiting our first point, your goals might be to increase this employee's level of performance, treat them fairly, and/or be open and honest in your communication. As a leader, you have a number of options in terms of how you manage this situation. Often the way we manage these situations is contingent upon our personal appraisals of what is happening. We will feel less compassion, for example, if we perceive that the employee has been given many opportunities to correct their behavior or if they are deliberately acting out. We might feel empathetic if the employee is dealing with a personal situation that is preventing them from performing to our expectations. This speaks to our assessment of their individual control of their circumstances.

From the perspective of the leader, knowing and being aware of our judgment and assessment is critical. Sometimes we want to treat everyone fairly, so we consciously attempt to ignore these aspects. However, I will challenge you to begin integrating the emotion and the perceived rationality. It is only in partnership that emotions and cognition lead you to the best decisions. Therefore, it is important to bring clarity and awareness to these judgments and use them to determine your personal emotional state. What elements are contributing to your assessment? How are your judgments impacting your emotional reaction?

Now, as a leader, you have two roles in this situation. Not only do you have to be aware of your goals and assessments, but you must also take into consideration the goals and assessments of your employees, because you are in the position of needing to take their emotional response into consideration. While you might feel frustrated, disappointed, and at your wits end with the situation, the employee might feel overwhelmed, fearful, and confused. Part of the role of the leader is to bring the emotions to a point of congruency. How can you arrive at a more neutral place and encourage your employee to take ownership of their own decisions and emotional experience? Ultimately, how can you make them accountable for their performance (hopefully increased performance)?

We can never achieve this outcome through fear. More often, we can accomplish this goal by having open communication about our feelings and arrive at common agreements, which we can hold our employees accountable for. When we do this, it begins to shape the emotional experience in a new way. We move from coercions and threats, which seek to control behavior but rarely do, to behaviors that connect to our employees' needs. We can create solid expectations and commitments, which, when not met, will allow the leader to address the situation in a new way and leave the leader and employee feeling much different. As opposed to the anger, frustration, and fear we might have experienced, we can move to a feeling of fairness, strength, and possibility. Our hope is that the outcome is increased performance, but even if it is not, we can have a different conversation about consequences—a conversation that leaves the employee and leader in a healthier place.

Therefore, when we consider these two variables (goals and appraisal), they work hand in hand to help us to determine what specific emotion will surface at any given time in any given situation. It also helps us to blend the rational, cognitive aspects of our nature with the emotional ones as we seek to feel and assess events. In considering the cognitive process of forming evaluations to given events, many of these appraisals occur relatively automatically. As one begins to process information, two types of cognition emerge: knowledge and appraisal. Knowledge is linked to what an individual infers about the cause of an event, potentially including aspects of who is at fault. Appraisal aligns to the assessment of the situation and relevance to the individual. At appraisal an individual might ask themselves, Do I care about this event? How does it impact me? Can I accept it? Will it get better or worse? These questions are posed in an effort to assess impact to personal well being[14]. The answers to these questions determine what emotion surfaces in any given situation.

As we react and respond, our emotional experiences are continuously being reevaluated, and different emotions emerge. As with our goals, these appraisals are continuous and will always change and feed new emotions. The question becomes, how do we as individuals judge a given event in terms of how it relates to our goals?

Activity

Consider a situation in which you and another person experienced the same event but had very different reactions. How did you assess the situation differently than the other person? What impact did assessment have in your varying reactions?

Consider a current challenge you are experiencing. What judgments are you making? How might those assessments be impacting your emotions about the situation? How about your decision making? Could you change your assessment in any way that would serve you? What appraisals are other people making regarding the same situation?

Lesson #3: Be Aware of Your Judgments, Appraisals, and Assessments

How we judge situations impacts our emotional experience and thus our reactions to various events. If we want to understand and manage our emotions, we must remain vigilantly aware of our personal judgments and assessments. As you become aware of your judgments, ask yourself the following:

1. Who am I blaming or assigning fault? Who do I see as responsible for the event? When we answer that question, "I am," we experience a much different emotion. What we find is when an event went well, we are more likely to take *responsibility* or credit. When the outcome of an event is seen as "not good," human nature tells us we must either accept responsibility ourselves or find someone else to blame. Unfortunately, it is often not safe in organizational environments to take responsibility, so we move to blame.

Who can be the scapegoat for this one? It is in those circumstances where we have diminished accountability and move into fear. All too often, we jump to blame before realizing that no one really needs to be at fault. Sometimes it's okay for no one to be blamed. In those moments, we seek learning and understanding. In those moments, we create trust.

As a leader, be cautious of how you assign blame. When you call out employees and place blame around various events or outcomes, you mistakenly increase fear and reduce your personal capacity and your employee's capacity for problem solving. A better alternative, when possible, is to depersonalize the situation, present the facts, and speak to the needed outcome. Ensure everyone is clear on their expectations and role. If someone is at fault, have that conversation with the individual in a way that supports their ability to assume ownership for their role in the situation.

2. What aspects of the situation do I have control over? When we think of fear, there is often a sense that we have no control. There is a general sense of high situational control—something beyond my control is creating this situation. With an emotion such as happiness, we might assume we have more control over the event. The more we can assume control or ownership of the situation and direct that control in a positive, productive way, the more we are able to move

from fear into emotions of challenge or hope—assuming ownership gives us power over our choices and decisions. It creates the necessary movement to keep us in a place of creativity and self-empowerment. When we resort to victim thinking and victim behavior, we might find ourselves relinquishing this control.

Continue to ask yourself, What control do I have? What aspects of this situation do I have the ability to change or influence? What options do I have, and how do I exercise those options? Exploring these questions will help you discover your own authority and power in all situations. Help your employees to explore these as well. When we are in a place of fear, we often go into fight-or-flight mode (which we will explore later). When we go into fight mode without being clear about our own ownership or control, we appear like a boxer who is swinging furiously but never even coming close to hitting his opponent. We are shooting the arrow from the bow with no target in sight. If we can feel the fear and get clear about our choices, options, and ownership, we can begin to fight from a place of strength and clarity.

The alternative, and more often the case, is we go into flight mode and shut down. We retreat into a place of perceived safety, and we hide. The problem with hiding is that we lose ourselves in that place. We lose our ability to be productive, to be creative, and to be whole. We no longer have the sense of what resources we need or how to call them forward. We become weak and broken. As employees and leaders, this is never an effective solution if we seek to meet personal or organizational objectives.

3. How much uncertainty does the situation hold? Fear encompasses a high level of uncertainty. When we do not know the outcome or create unlikely outcomes (like unrealistic worst-case scenarios), we can increase our fear response. The more certainty we can provide, the less fear will result. When we consider this from the perspective of a leader, we must consider delivering information that will help people to be more certain. In the absence of information, leaders and employees will create it. We develop elaborate what-if scenarios—generally negative stories about how terrible the outcome could be. How often have you jumped to the worst-case scenario, knowing that the probability of that event was very low? Nevertheless, we make these leaps all the time, and sometimes we grab others as we're jumping. This is often called the rumor mill.

The more leaders can reduce uncertainty for their staff, the less likely they will be to move into fear. Likewise, the more you can reduce your own personal uncertainty, the less likely you personally will move into fear. As a leader, when you help employees avoid fear and increase their certainty, you are actually enabling them to spend their energy working toward a solution, as opposed to constructing these elaborate what-if scenarios that will never happen.

As we seek to understand emotions and the emotion of fear, we can begin to see how these intricacies surface and develop in our lives. By knowing the goal and being aware of your judgments, you can begin to not only understand your emotional experience but develop the capacity to alter, manage, and regulate your resulting actions..

Emotions Are Critical for Our Survival

We now know that emotions result from our individual goals and what we want to accomplish in any given encounter or circumstance. They are impacted by our appraisals and judgments and influenced by who we are and what we value. If our goal shifts, so do our emotional responses. If our assessment of the situation shifts, so does our emotional response. If our awareness of values, personality, and motivational needs becomes heighted, it can influence our emotional reaction.

A final premise for the understanding of emotions, particularly fear, is that emotions have an evolutionary role, and they are linked to our ability to survive[15]. Emotional theorists will often speak to the notion of basic, primary, or instinctual emotions. Some would argue that fear and love are the foundation of all emotion. Others have suggested anger, fear, and sadness. Most models also include shame, surprise, and joy. Fear, however, is pivotal in all these models, demonstrating that at a primal level fear instinctually guides our decision making from a place so deep that we struggle to control it.

As we consider fear throughout the remainder of the book, recognizing the primal nature of fear can be important. We've discussed all the variables impacting emotion, such as values, goals, and appraisal, but with fear, these elements occur and surface at such a basic level it can often be difficult to consciously and cognitively integrate the experience fast enough to know what has happened. When you see a bear in the woods, your survival instinct of fear kicks into gear, and you react. When your child runs toward a busy street, your fear sets in, and you immediately respond. The same is true for our workplace fears. We often feel the fear in our bodies long before our cognitive assessment and conscious awareness has caught up.

As we consider emotions and our survival, we are also taking into account whether we can cope with the demands a given situation has presented. If we determine we can cope well with the event, we might begin to feel a sense of invigoration or challenge. If we believe we are unable to cope, we fall into a different emotional spectrum—feeling fearful, paralyzed, and frustrated.

John's story:

I met John one fall season as I was working with his organization on a culture assessment. John was a stellar performer at the organization. His leadership was strong, and his results were consistently high. In talking with employees, they shared that John had high expectations, and they all loved working for him. They cared about him so much that they never wanted to disappoint him. They worked hard as a team, and they worked hard for him. His division had been the top performing in the company for nearly five years, and his leadership was being noticed throughout the organization. John's team felt appreciated, respected, and loyal. John felt proud, accomplished, and confident.

Within months, John had an opportunity to move into a larger division with more responsibility (and more money). He had succeeded previously in turning around a very difficult situation, and the organization wanted him to lead them through another challenge. As John stepped into the new role, he did what he knew how to do. He displayed honesty, had high expectations, and demonstrated strength. His team felt fearful, angry, and resentful.

John began to struggle getting results. He had a desire for outcomes, and so he increased the sense of urgency. His people were always on edge and felt the pressure not as a challenge to do better but as a threat that if they did worse, they might lose their jobs. John's manager was getting concerned that perhaps they put him in over his head. Maybe he couldn't handle this situation. Maybe they choose the wrong guy. John's feelings began to turn to paranoia, anger, and fear—fear he might lose his job, fear that he was looking incompetent, fear that he didn't belong. His employees also felt pressured, hopeless, and fearful.

The common thread is always fear. John's story demonstrates, at a more complex level, how we experience emotion relative to a goal. John's goal was always to be successful and achieve results. However, as he changed situations, the emotions shifted as he moved closer or further away from that goal. He also shifted in his emotional experience as his ability to cope with the situation changed.

What Does It Mean in Our Working Lives?

The interesting element of emotions lies in their complexity. We now know that the same event can trigger a different emotional reaction depending on our individual goals and personal appraisal of the situation. Given this, we are left in a bit of a quandary as we seek to not only navigate our own emotions but support our employees in navigating theirs. As we understand more about what leads to emotion and the various components of emotion, we can begin to refine how we engage in various situations with employees (or even ourselves) in order to better manage the emotional experience.

As leaders, we must balance two perspectives. It becomes critical that we have awareness and regulate our own emotions, because our emotions contribute to the appraisal our staff makes when they begin the process of expressing and evaluating their own emotions.

An important point of note as we consider the foundation of emotions in the workplace is to know that negative emotions will narrow people's thoughts and actions. These emotions will result in individuals acting in ways they deem acceptable or prescribed. Alternatively, positive emotions expand the range of behavioral options and promote thinking and actions that are more creative and out of the box. As leaders, what do you want from your staff?

What Do We Desire in Our Working Lives?

So what does this all mean for us as employees? As leaders? It means we need greater consciousness about the role emotions—and particularly fear—play in our workplaces and our personal lives. How are these emotions impacting us? How are they impacting our decisions? How are they impacting others around us? Increasing our awareness will allow us to consciously determine if a given goal or emotion is serving us and our employees. It will help us determine if we need to do something the same or different. If I know I feel joy and excitement when I get to work on a certain type of project, I need to be aware and continue to move toward that type of work. If something drains me, I need to know that as well so I can avoid it.

We often find ourselves relinquishing so much power to others over our lives. This enhanced understanding of our own emotions, desires, and reactions will place us in control of our destination. It puts you in the driver's seat of your own progress and happiness. It helps you retain your own personal power.

As we consider the variables and drivers of emotions, we can begin to gain perspective on how these surface in relation to fear. The next chapter begins to outline the nature of fear and what we can expect from our fear— predictable causes and reactions that surface from our emotional state. Understanding the basics of emotion can also aid us in developing strategies to minimize fear in our leadership, teams, and organizations.

THE NATURE OF FEAR

I remember as a sophomore in high school having to take a required swimming class called Drownproofing. While I could swim, I was deathly afraid of the water. More specifically, I feared being *in* the water, and even more specifically than that, I was scared at the thought of having to put my face into the water. That feeling of water in my nose, no ability to take a necessary breath, the pressure of the water above me—it made me physically ill. I was petrified, and I found myself seeking all sorts of creative options to avoid it—even dropping out of high school all together. I found myself thinking, *Who really needed high school anyway?*

It all seems so ridiculous now when I think back on it. Of all the things to be afraid of, why that? Surely there were more important fears—and there were. Yet in all those cases, my body took over, and no amount of rationality was going to convince me that I had nothing to be afraid of. We all have these stories, be they incidents of abuse and trauma or seemingly silly circumstances of dread. The fears we face as children remain as we enter our work lives. Despite changing situations, the physical and emotional response feels the same. It hits us when we least expect it and takes over uncontrollably.

Meet Jennifer:

Jennifer was a mid-level manager who worked in the retail environment. Her story will be familiar to many of you as it speaks to the common moments we face as leaders in organizations.

> I am sitting in the boardroom, staring at twenty of the most serious faces I have ever seen. I crack a joke to lighten the mood, but there will be no softening of spirits here. Profits are down, market share is falling, quality is declining, and employee engagement is plummeting. I have been asked to speak before senior leadership and present my department's scorecard. Our performance is no better than the rest of the organization. We are struggling in the same ways as other leaders. I sit at the head of a long, dark conference table. There are seven senior leaders on either side of the table, and I just watched the person in front of me, a peer and friend, leave the room stiff and sterile. Every hour on the hour, leaders have entered and left the room. One by one we are each asked to explain our budget and present a plan for improvement. One by one we are all put on the stand.
>
> My mouth is so dry I can hardly speak. I can feel my heart pounding through my chest, and I remember wondering if anyone could see it beating through my suit jacket. My stomach is in knots, and I am at a loss for words. On this

day, I am interrogated by my leadership. I feel so defensive as they attack me with questions. I defend myself; I defend my staff. Yet I am left wondering—there must be a better way to lead. There must be a better way to achieve results.

Fear Is Primal

All living things feel fear. It is primal and instinctual. We react to our fear long before we even know it. It's like a fire that starts with a small spark, and suddenly the flames are engulfing you. But like a fire, we can gain control of the burn. We can allow the spark to serve as a warning sign, and we can find water to squelch the blaze.

Our fear is our basic protection mechanism—our reaction to threat, our defense from harm. It has kept us alive and allowed us to thrive in the face of adversity. Fear was never meant to be a way of life. It was meant to be a sign of caution to keep us safe from harm. How, then, have we arrived at this place where fear encompasses us, permeating every fiber of our being?

I often ask clients who are stuck in fear, "What is the opposite of fear?" Their response varies from love to courage; trust to safety; confidence to acceptance, peace, and faith. I wonder what your response would be to that question. How would you define the opposite of fear? Would it vary depending on our situation? I find that the answer speaks to our needs in those moments of fear. When the response is love, you might ask yourself whether the situation you are currently in demands a loving approach. If you respond with the answer of safety, that might be exactly what you are requiring. When we believe the opposite of fear is courage, we likely need to find ways to bring more bravery into our situation.

Our world is filled with fear. We are living in difficult times, which require us, more than ever, to seek fear's companion. As I look around me, fear is open, and fear is clouded. It is obvious, and it is hidden. Sometimes we are clear about our fears, and other times we are uncertain. Often our fears are conscious, and frequently they are hidden deep within the unconscious. As we think about fear, we must attentively seek its companion—it's seemingly opposite. It is only in those places—places of hope and love, places of safety and trust, courage and faith—that we can truly understand fear and know how to be with it in a way that serves us and those around us—those who we lead, those who we follow, those who we love.

The Spark:
What Are You Afraid Of?

What is it? Whether we call it fear, anxiety, worry, apprehension, nervousness, or doubt—what is it for you? What are you afraid of? (Feel free to check all that apply.)

- ☐ Losing your job?
- ☐ Being yelled at?
- ☐ Having someone disapprove of you?
- ☐ Failing?
- ☐ Succeeding?

- ☐ Moving through change?
- ☐ Speaking up in meetings?
- ☐ Asserting yourself?
- ☐ Experiencing conflict?
- ☐ Being stuck?
- ☐ Losing your voice?
- ☐ Making decisions?
- ☐ Making the wrong decisions?
- ☐ Changing careers?
- ☐ Looking foolish in front of others?

The Cause of Fear

Regardless of what we fear, at the core fear is always about threat—the feeling of danger, the unknown, or a negative consequence. Fear is one of the most basic emotions experienced, not only by humans, but also by all animals. Fear is always our reaction to a real or perceived danger. I emphasize the word *perceived* very deliberately. The old saying "Perception is reality" becomes critical in this case.

This summer, my home became a migration pattern for reptiles. I had turtles, toads, and snakes crossing my path everyday. One day late in the season, we found two large bull snakes in the yard. My husband picked them up with the intention of relocating them to a field next to a nearby river. The first one was easy to scoop up and place in the bucket. Scared and threatened, it coiled up and buried its head into itself. The second was more aggressive. It hissed and fought, tried to bite, and lashed its body in fear. Although two very different reactions, both were instinctual responses to the animals' fear, a threat they were experiencing to their very survival. One went into fight mode, working to protect itself, and the other flight, trying to hide in order to maintain safety.

This example provides a nice introduction to the concept of fear, but it also allows us to see how perception of threat is just as real as the actual threat. From the example above, the snake was never in real danger. We had no intention of hurting it in any way. We actually wanted to keep it safe. However, it reacted based on a perception of threat, which was equally as real as a genuine threat would have been.

As people, we operate the same way. I hear clients frequently share stories. They speak of times when they were called into the boss's office. Their first reaction, generally without any reason to substantiate it, is, "Am I in trouble?"

We often jump to the conclusion of threat. Why don't we ever wonder, "Am I getting promoted?" or, "I bet they want to add a large bonus to my next paycheck," or even, "You are doing a great job, and I want to acknowledge it"?

Instinctually, we jump to threat. Often this is a result of previous experiences we may have had in similar situations or societal learning around expectations, and sometimes it surfaces from the unknown.

These reactions are not that different from our own response as leaders and employees. How often, when presented with the threats and fears listed above, do we engage in either a flight or flight strategy? Sometimes we come out swinging, not even sure where we're aiming, and sometimes we look for a hole to bury our head in.

The Purpose of Fear in Our Lives

Fear is a safety mechanism, a warning system designed to alert us to a threat, get our attention, and move us a different direction (away from the danger). Whether we elect to engage our fight-or-flight response, this internal alarm was designed to protect us from harm. Unfortunately, in our workplaces (and our lives, for that matter), fear has become a regular partner for us. As I pulled up the Internet today, I read about elevated security levels due to terrorist threats, mass lay-offs expected throughout the country as the economic crisis worsens, and another school shooting. Fear is meant to be a signal of caution, designed to tell us when we are in danger. It was never meant to be a state of being. When it becomes a state of being, it loses its effectiveness as an alarm. What we seek, then, is a way to become consciously aware of those *real* fears, manage the perceived fears in a different way, and be more in tune to the signal that fear was designed to be.

As we seek to strike a balance between real and perceived threats, we have to learn to tell the difference between the real fear that we should be paying attention to and the unhealthy fear that might actually prevent us from learning and growing. As leaders, we can't project our irrational fears onto others. It's not helpful for them or us. As employees, we need to get clear about what we are afraid of and seek to actively resolve it.

Meet Linda:

It was an early afternoon, a warm summer day with expected rain. I had just returned from a business trip that morning and walked into Bruce's office. Bruce was the chief executive officer for the company—a large man who seemed intimidating to others but with whom I had always had a good relationship. As I entered the room, the conversation seemed natural and normal.

"How are you doing? What are your plans for the holiday?"

Rapidly, the energy in the room began to shift. The details of the experience and issue seemed less relevant at this point than the raw fear I could feel pulsing through my entire body as the conversation proceeded. My heart began to pound, and my mouth went dry as I tried to understand what was occurring. I found myself confused, fearful, and frustrated. I had a great deal of uncertainty, and the outcome for me personally was unknown. The experience of raw fear permeated every ounce of my being.

Why fear?

In Linda's situation above, she entered the conversation with no reason to feel afraid. Her goals were not at risk, and she was not in a position that required her to avoid harm. As the conversation continued, however, her emotional experience shifted as well. With further discussion and changing events, she began to realize that her goals, including keeping her job and maintaining her integrity, were at risk, and her subsequent emotion was fear.

Throughout a thirty-minute meeting, the emotions she experienced were great—ranging from joy, friendliness, and openness to confusion, frustration, and fear.

As we've discussed, fear exists as a physical mechanism to protect us and keep us secure. It triggers us to avoid or address certain threats that confront us. Fear can occur within organizations for a variety of reasons—including fear of job loss and loss of power and/or control, failure, success, uncertainty, punishment, changes, decision making, and risk taking. Whether we call it fear or use some other word like anxiety, nervousness, or worry, it stems from the same basic need and often has the same result.

As mentioned earlier, our action tendency in fear is either fight or flight. In the work setting, this might appear to be an aggressive reaction to a situation or a deep shrinking and avoidance. We will explore these two reactions more, but when we think about the result in the organizational environment, neither of these reactions, particularly at their extreme, is healthy as we seek innovation, engagement, and results.

In the previous chapter, we discussed the drivers of emotion. The connection between motivation and emotion is significant. Motivation helps us to understand what causes behavior. It also lies at the core of our emotional experience. Our decision making, judgments, and behavioral tendencies are linked to our motivational desires. Remember that our motivation impacts our goals, and our goals drive our emotions. When we feel our goals are at risk or when they are being threatened, we will enter a place of fear. We will feel motivated to avoid harm (threat) and react in a behavioral way to ensure our own protection.

When we begin to think about fear and what specific situations or events cause fear, an understanding of our basic motivational needs becomes foundational. A classic psychological motivational theorist Abraham Maslow presented a hierarchy of needs that outlines five basic levels of human needs. The illustration below describes these five levels. As we learn more about what motivates us personally and professionally, we can look to the hierarchy to define levels of development. Other organizational theorists have presented additional work around motivation. Fredrick Herzberg proposed a two-factor theory or motivator/hygiene theory to better understand workplace motivators and dissatisfers[16].

Hierarchy of Needs

Activity

Consider what motivates you at work. Is it money and benefits, the contribution you make, the ability to help others, or status? Perhaps it is important that you be able to bring forward your skills and expertise and be recognized for that knowledge. Again, there are no right or wrong answers. We are driven by any combination of motivators. Knowing these key motivators can be critical as we seek to determine where threats surface in relation to fear. This knowledge can also aid us in determining other emotional states that might serve us.

My key motivators:

_____

_____

_____

The idea of motivation becomes relevant and critical in our discussion of fear. It sets the context as to what generates the perception of threat and subsequently, fear. When motivational aspects that we hold important are in danger, we will respond with fear. In the remainder of this chapter, we will discuss threats to our security and safety, affiliation, and self-esteem. In the workplace, these are the greatest areas that generate threat. They reflect the second, third, and fourth level of Maslow's hierarchy of needs.

In the organizational environment, we need employees that can respond in self-actualized ways (whether they are truly self-actualized is another question). What we desire are employees that can engage in their work creatively and individuals who can effectively problem solve and support organizational efforts. If we adhere to the motivational theory of Maslow's hierarchy of needs, then we might assume that employees cannot reach their full potential unless their lower-level needs are addressed. These would include security, safety, belonging, and self-esteem. As leaders, it is our role to create environments that meet lower-level needs in order to allow our employees to fully show up from a greater place.

The Gallup Organization conducted a significant amount of research on this topic and created a model, which in many ways reflects the Maslow's hierarchy. The Gallup Q12 engagement survey helps organizations to better understand these needs, specifically as they impact employee engagement. At the base of their pyramid lie questions about what employees get from their work environment and how the company meets their basic needs. Do they have the materials and equipment they need? Do they know what is expected of them? Moving up the pyramid, the survey assesses their senses of belonging, contribution, and ability to grow[17].

As we consider these aspects of motivation, we can begin to see the various places where threat can occur. I recently worked with a leader who had been promoted within the last six months. At that time in her career, it was important to her that she show senior leadership she had the right information, always knew what was happening, and was able to make all the right suggestions. This was motivating her at this time. When those aspects of her leadership were threatened, she went into fear and unconsciously used that fear with others on her team. Let's spend some time discussing where threats come from.

The Flame: Where Is the Threat Coming From?

It seems worth repeating. Fear comes from threats to our basic human needs[18]. This being the case, what motivates us also helps us to understand these needs and various fears we experience around them. In relation to fear in the workplace, we experience fears primarily in three areas of the hierarchy—threats to security, threats to affiliation, and threats to self-esteem.

Drivers of Fear

The sections that follow will use stories to discuss these various areas of fear. As you read the stories, consider your own experiences. While this section merely presents the fears, along with the stories, the following chapter will outline the language of fear and discuss those specific leadership behaviors that induce fear.

Threats to Our Existence, Safety, and Security

Safety Threats

Threats to safety answer questions such as, Will I be fired? Is my job secure? What are my working conditions? Am I safe at work? Am I making enough money to survive? Are my benefits adequate?

Below, I have included a number of examples where individuals experienced fear as a result of threats to their security needs. As you read these stories, consider your own experiences of fear resulting from security threats. Have you personally had experiences such as these? Have you created these experiences for your employees? What is your role as a leader in managing these emotional experiences and threats to the safety and security needs of your employees?

Meet Emma:

> My situations of fear generally involved potential
> or actual violence at work. I feel like I needed

to be a security guard with all the physically abusive situations I found myself dealing with. When I was a new supervisor, I was the only women on a night team. My director had hired a gentleman, and from the beginning he made me feel uncomfortable. He said he knew where I lived and he would have to stop over some time. I was very afraid of him. He was terminated, and about two months later, I read in the paper that the police had found a dead body in the trunk of his car. It was a frightening experience and left me wondering how I listen to my intuition to keep myself safe.

On another occasion, I had recently assumed a director role. I had an employee who was about six foot four and probably weighed two hundred and ninety pounds. All of my employees were afraid of him. I didn't quite understand why at first. Over time, however, I came to discover that he was telling other employees that he had beaten up an employee at his other job and gotten fired. His behavior and verbal aggression frightened the team. They worried for their physical safety.

Emma's examples demonstrate the nature of physical threats in our work environments. They speak to the various situations that we might unknowingly place our employees in. When we think about our role as leaders in creating a safe environment for our staff, it's important to remember that these types of situations do occur—more frequently than we want to believe. Below, Sam shares his experience.

Meet Sam:

> I am a front-line manager. I have an excellent department, but sometimes we get people in that create significant fear for my team and me. I had a worker that came to my office. He stood in the doorway, blocking the entrance.
>
> He was very menacing, saying, "What are you going to do? I could hurt you right now, and there is nothing you could do about it."
>
> The verbal words felt threatening, and certainly his non-verbal behaviors contributed to it.

If we adhere to the hierarchy of motivational needs, we can understand the importance of having safe work environments and feeling secure at work. Verbal and non-verbal threats can leave us in a place of discomfort and fear. As you read the examples below, consider your own experiences and whether you have had similar situations.

Meet Joshua:

> As a manager, I am dealing with these situations all the time. I typically perform turnaround work, which means I take poorly performing, problematic departments and try to make them better. Often, you make hard decisions in these situations—decisions people don't like, and

it can make them angry and vengeful. I have had employees threaten me at work and send letters to my home. When I tried to deal with the situation, there were a lot of fears in the organization about legal action. As a leader, it makes it difficult sometimes to do your job. You feel like your hands are tied.

From these conversations with leaders, I learned that situations of conflict consistently created threat and fear for leaders and employees. Disciplinary conversations can be one of the most challenging aspects of leadership. The ability to engage in these difficult conversations without fear can be challenging. As we think about strategies to reduce these types of fears, it is important we obtain support as a pivotal success factor in these types of situations. Often, leaders seek to have other people present or at least know they are supported in their decision in order to reduce their fear. The other thing to remember is that while the leader is fearful, the employee is experiencing significant fear as well. While both individuals have different threats generating the fear, responses can be consistent.

Meet Amanda:

I didn't think I would ever experience this. It's still difficult to talk about—almost shameful in some way, but I had an experience of sexual harassment. I remember being so afraid, not only of losing my job, but of people finding out. I worried that it would somehow be considered my fault. It took me a while to realize what was happening. It occurred gradually over time. I didn't know what to do, who to turn to, or who I could trust. This person was over me in the hierarchy, and in the environment I was in, you didn't buck the system of power.

Amanda's example brings in elements of power and control that can significantly impact our level of fear. Anytime we perceive a lack of control over our circumstances, the sense of fear is heightened. Additionally, when we perceive someone to have power (either personal or position power) over us and those things we value, we will have an elevated sense of fear. In both these situations, dynamics of power occurred that played a significant role on how the leader and employee experience and project fear.

As we consider these stories of physical threat or unsafe environments, most leaders would argue that it is our job to create a safe environment for employees. It's also our job not to use threatening tactics with our staff. When we raise our voice, display fits of anger, or use intimidation and bullying tactics, we elevate fear. In these cases, the risk is not only increased fear in our staff, but we hold liability from a legal and employment risk perspective as well.

When this environment exists in our organizations or departments, it must be immediately squelched. There are countless books on workplace violence and bullying, so I don't want to go into a great amount of detail here. The main point worthy of note is that fear in the workplace is often generated by physical threat—real or perceived. As we consider our role as leaders, along with the concept of workplace bullying, the perceived threat can be just as significant. If you engage in behaviors, intentionally or unintentionally, that could be perceived as threatening, the risk is present.

Activity

- Have you ever felt physically threatened or unsafe at work? What were the circumstances?

  _____

- As a leader, would you ever be perceived as threatening by any of your staff?

  _____

- What specific behaviors do you engage in that might be viewed as aggressive?

  _____

- Do you ensure safe work environments? Are there areas where you are at risk?

  _____

- How can you create a safer work environment?

- How might you change your behaviors to do so?

Security Threats

Another aspect of threat at this level is threats to our job security. Fear of job loss is one of the primary drivers of workplace fear. In every interview I have conducted around fear, fear of being fired or let go from a job surfaces at some point in the discussion. As we think about motivation, we must recognize that real or perceived threats of job loss have a significant impact to employee's job performance and morale. When employees have financial security and job retention, their personal security needs are met. This threat strikes at the core of our ability to survive. Often, this threat runs so deep into our psyche that we create stories, make assumptions, and become paralyzed at the mere thought of losing our income and employment. This impact becomes exacerbated if employees have had previous experience with termination or lay-offs.

The impact of threats to our job security is great. When we fear so deeply in this arena, we actually will contract upon ourselves unknowingly. We collapse, and our performance suffers precisely at those moments when we need to improve most. We might make more errors, we are less capable of problem solving, and our physical health is negatively impacted. Since this threat is so core to our being, threats to job security will often also create the greatest fight-or-flight protection reaction. Leaders are challenged to manage these difficult situations with ease and grace in order to keep themselves and their employees capable and whole. Below are several different stories to paint the picture of security fears.

Meet Edward:

> I am currently self-employed, and about a year ago I was laid off from a company I worked with for twenty years. Losing my job was the worst fear that I had ever experienced. My fear became a reality. I felt helpless and powerless to change my situation. Now, I am on my own with my business, and there's still fear around not having enough money to survive.
>
> I am always creating these "what if" scenarios. What if I don't succeed? What if I don't get work? What if I can't pay my bills and support my family? There was total fear. For me, security was about having money, and if I didn't have that, than I'm not safe. The fear was about loss—fear of losing finances, fear of losing social status, and fear of being emotionally alone.

Meet Scott:

> I had recently accepted a new leadership role. About six months into the position, the company chose to bring in an external consultant to assess

whether certain positions should be eliminated. Trust was low, and the ultimate threat for me was job loss. I knew a severance package wouldn't last long, and I found myself deeply worried about being let go. I feared for the financial loss, but I also was afraid of how I would find something else in this challenging economy.

Meet Cassandra:

In my current company, if you get a written warning of any kind, there are negative consequences. It will affect many of your benefits, and you can't transfer to another department. If you get a written warning, you are stuck. Sometimes, the fear of staying is worse than the fear of being fired. I always find myself worrying about what I say. What if I say something and I get disciplined? What if I do something that gets me fired? What if I say something and people don't like me? I am the best "what-ifer."

The stories above reflect fears of job loss and are just a few of the many that I have compiled over years of consulting and coaching. Perhaps you can see yourself in some of these examples. I wonder what your stories would tell. I personally can speak of many occasions where I was afraid of losing my position. This fear held significant negative consequences for me. Despite the strength I think I have created, this fear continues to be one of my ongoing battles with fear. I want to be able to tell myself that I'm not afraid of losing my income—that I trust everything would be okay, that I could surrender to a greater purpose. I want to be able to say those things, but like all my interviewees, when confronted with this reality...I am scared.

Our job security is foundational. Unfortunately, we will put up with abuse, unhappiness, and lack of fulfillment to ensure we are secure. We will compromise ourselves and our inner truth in order to meet this basic human need. Our employees will tolerate a poor leader and a horrible organization in order to support themselves and their loved ones.

As a leader, however, I can assure you that you are not getting the best from your employees if they are concerned about job loss. We can feel the fear of security so deep in our bodies it can create physical illness. We might call it stress or burnout, but it manifests in our physical nature. Heart issues, stomach problems, and shakiness can all be symptoms of deep fear.

I encourage you to consider whether your employees are fearful for their jobs. Are you? When leaders and employees experience fear for their jobs, they will display varying behaviors, including silence, absenteeism, or outbursts of anger. If individuals are well developed personally and exhibit high self-awareness, they might assume ownership of their piece of the situation. They will identify aspects of the situation within their control and make positive movement in the direction required. Most often however, they will engage in blame, defensiveness, and rage. Consider if you are witnessing any of these demeanors in yourself or your team members.

As a leader, managing these behaviors is a core responsibility, and often one of our greatest challenges. If we can pause and seek understanding about why employees are behaving this way, we can often begin to create discussions that support employees, thereby minimizing their defensive, fear-based response. Remember that fear results from the unknown and feeling limited control over our circumstances. The more we can minimize these two variables, the more we can decrease fear and the negative behaviors that surface as a result. Have open communications with your staff. Try to be as transparent as possible. Be supportive and allow them to express their concerns and fears.

As we seek to lead, we are often placed in positions where we have to make difficult determinations about our employees and their performance. When we have a difficult employee, leaders often struggle with whether their assessment about this person is correct. The important question leaders battle is whether they are making the right decision—are they making the right call? Leaders deal with low performers. Leaders must sometimes downsize or restructure in ways that eliminate employees. It is an unfortunate and often excruciatingly painful part of the job. The key question is not whether you need to engage in performance conversations or move forward with a strategy that requires lay-offs or termination—the real question is how you carry out those conversations and decisions. So, I ask you, what is within your control? How can you maintain a high level of integrity in those discussions? How can you be transparent, honest, and compassionate? How can you support your employees through fear of job security?

Employees who are fearful for their job security (real or perceived) need open, honest communication and frequent feedback. If you have an employee who is unrealistically fearful, provide them regular, positive feedback about their strong performance. Establish agreements in terms of communication about their gaps. In this way, they will know what to expect when their performance is not meeting expectations. For those employees who are not performing up to standards, have those discussions as well. Be open, honest, and realistic. Coach them. Ask them powerful questions that encourage them to own their role. Transparency is highly effective and requires that you continue to deliver feedback.

One final point to consider: often times, an organizational symptom of this fear is low retention and high turnover. We might also see higher than usual errors or mistakes from employees in fear. If people are in fear and believe they are at risk, they will take control of their destinies and seek employment elsewhere. However, in a changing economy, this can be masked as individuals are unable to find other options. Reviewing your retention data can provide insights into whether you are operating in a culture of fear in terms of safety and security.

Activity

What experiences have you had where you were afraid of losing your job?

_____

_____

Does your organization have a culture of fear? Are you a fear-based leader?

_____

_____

How might you approach performance conversations differently to reduce fear?

_____

_____

Threats to Our Sense of Affiliation

The next category of threat based on the hierarchy of personal needs centers around threats to affiliation. We have a basic human desire for belonging, feeling connected to groups, and having social affiliations that align to our values and make us feel a part of something. Leaders often say, "I would rather be respected than liked." While it makes a great quote on the wall, it minimizes the reality of our need to be liked and a part of something. As we consider various leadership principles, they often speak to making everyone feel part of the team, valuing all contributions, and inspiring the team to perform. We cannot underestimate our basic human need to be part of a team—to be liked and respected and to contribute in a way that confirms our personal value.

I worked with a CEO a few years ago who was a tough, fair man who spoke his truth and stood strong in difficult professional decisions. Often, as you can imagine, when we make those difficult choices, it can result in hard feelings toward you by others.

One day in my office, as he was discussing one of these very difficult choices, he stated, "Deep down, I really do want to be liked, and it feels horrible getting beat up like this."

While we might try to hide it, and we often deny our needs around them, affiliation fears can be the cause of many performance problems. Most companies have strong on-boarding strategies. They work hard to make people feel a part of the company and often establish buddy programs to help new staff acclimate. When we see employees who turn over in the few months of hire, it is often a result of affiliation needs not being met. We might also see this in group dysfunction when conflict results in fighting and deep dissension amongst group members. These issues will result in decreased outcomes and low trust[19].

As painful as it might be, remember back to junior high or high school. Recall the devastation of not being selected to be part of a team—the difficulty when you fought with your friends and were on the outside of the group or the humiliation you felt when you knew people were talking behind your back. It seems ridiculous that we bring these behaviors and emotions forward into our adult life, but they are human nature. It is part of our human experience. In the workplace, it shows up as conversation or gossip behind people's backs, a sense of being ignored or not included, or even intentionally "forgetting" to invite someone to meetings. For the CEO that I spoke about above, it was everyone talking and sharing their frustration behind his back, leaving the lunchroom abruptly when he was walking near, and his general knowledge that people didn't like him for the decisions he made.

In regard to this issue, I've heard comments like, "In leadership, it's not my job to be everyone's friend. I have to make the tough decisions. That is what I am paid for."

I am not suggesting that leadership is a popularity contest. What I am saying is that despite how we rationalize the issue of affiliation, we all have a foundational need to be part of something and to feel a sense of belonging. As leaders, when we don't create that and meet that need for employees, they will enter a place of fear, and we will ultimately experience the consequences as an organization.

The stories below seek to demonstrate some of the ways that fears from threats to our sense of affiliation surface for leaders and employees. Consider these examples and ask yourself when you have been in situations where you performed better because you were part of a team you enjoyed. When have you shown up stronger because someone connected to your need for belonging and you felt appreciated?

Meet Brian:

> When I started my new job, I knew there would be a lot to learn. It was so helpful when I was greeted by a peer and partnered with someone for the first two weeks. Everyone on my team was so willing to help me.
>
> Everyone kept affirming, "We are so glad you are here. We have heard so many good things about you."
>
> I was introduced to all the people I would be working with. They invited me to lunch. They showed appreciation, and it made me feel much more comfortable. I've been in new jobs in the past where you come in and you are on your own. You have to figure out where your space is, how to get a computer, who is who. It's awful. There is definitely less fear when you start in an environment that is welcoming and you feel you belong and have a connection with people.

Meet Melissa:

> I am a front-line leader. I have to manage operations, schedules, and workflow on a daily basis. I am always afraid I will make a decision

people don't like, and then they will be upset with me. I am told it's part of my job and I shouldn't care what others think, but the truth is, I do care. I want to make decisions that people like, and the conflict I experience bothers me. It makes me fearful, not of losing my job, but of straining my work relationships. And when my work relationships are strained, I don't enjoy work, which makes it hard to want to come in and do a good job.

As leaders, we take two lessons from these stories. First, be vulnerable to considering your own needs around affiliation, belonging, and social affiliation in the workplace. Second, be aware that your employees have these needs as well, and when they are not met, they will be in a place of fear and threat. We don't often use the word *love* in regard to our work environment, but consider where you need to lead from love in order to create environments of support and belonging.

As I listen to people talk about their fears around belonging, there is almost a sense of shame or denial. They frequently share comments like, "I know I shouldn't get upset about this," or, "It shouldn't make feel this way, but…"

It is such a gift for me to be able to hear and share these stories. This belief that we shouldn't have certain feelings or emotions is something we all need to let go of. Anytime the word *should* (in any form—including *should not*) surfaces in your vocabulary, it's time to reassess and determine where it's coming from. *Should* often represents interpreted obligations that are not our own; they belong to someone else. If you're upset, be upset. Feel the emotion and work through it. Don't allow yourself to apologize for being who you are and experiencing what you are feeling. Be with it. Appreciate it. Take the message from it. Act on it.

Applying this four-step formula can be powerful for both yourself and your employees. Affirming emotions that surround lack of affiliation is important. Leaders must also create environments that foster inclusion. Not everyone on your team will be best friends. Various personalities and styles will likely result in some team members engaging in closer relationships than others. However, establishing a team environment which is collegial and noncompetitive can be key factors in ensuring that employees feel a sense of belonging. Pay attention to signs that your workplace may be cliché' or divided. If you notice subgroups forming on your team, consider partnering different employees together on projects or work efforts. You might also benefit from teambuilding or training which helps employees value their personality differences.

If you have employees voicing concerns that they just don't fit in or feel left out, don't dismiss these claims as immature or petty. Hear them and act on them. Also, assist employees in determining what is within their control to do differently. How can they more proactively engage teammates in relationship building? As leaders, we all too often want to dismiss these complaints, but I encourage you strongly to pay attention. Issues of belonging, when not addressed, can have dire consequences, including significant human-resources complaints, employment lawsuits and workplace violence.

Activity

What does your outcome data show you in terms of potential fears? What is your turnover rate? What is your employee engagement/satisfaction rate?

_____

_____

What are you personal needs for belonging and affiliation? Where are you feeling left out or not a part of something in the way you'd like to be?

_____

_____

What are your employees experiencing? Are they feeling a sense of belonging to the team? Do they feel a part of something?

_____

_____

What are you actively doing to create affiliation for your staff?

_____

_____

Threats to Our Ego and Self-Esteem

As I have conducted interviews on fear in the workplace, I typically find that threats to security (job loss, physical safety) are felt at the most visceral level. They seem to be core to our beings and provide the strongest fight-or-flight reaction. They quickly and instinctually move us into responses of paralysis, feelings of being stuck and having no choice, or battling fiercely for our own survival. When we begin to move up the hierarchy to those situations that generate a threat to our self-esteem, the tone of the discussion begins to shift. We start to hear a vulnerability that reflects a deeper part of who we are. Threats at this level touch a side of us that reflects perceived weakness and a rawness of our being. We start to question whether we are good enough, strong enough, or capable enough. Our self-confidence and doubt of that confidence come into play.

We see it throughout history. Moses pleaded with God that perhaps he wasn't the right one to lead the people from Egypt. Mother Theresa questioned her personal strength to fulfill her calling. Ghandi, Martin Luther King, Buddha, and Abraham Lincoln—the list could go on, but one thing remains true: all great leaders have experienced fear and felt powerless at the very core of their being. One differentiating factor is that great leaders move through the fear and remain true to themselves and their calling.

Threats to our self-esteem strike at our very soul—the very nature of who are and who we seek to be. They are damaging and strengthening all at the same time. They can bring us to our knees or inspire us to rise up and fight for our very essence. These fears can easily cause us to go against our principles and compromise our values, or they can create alignment between our character and our actions. As we think about this in light of basic psychology, we know our ego deals with the realities in our life circumstances, and it supports our ability to create equilibrium between what we want and what is our best course of action. Fears in this arena signify a complex web of balancing our personal desires with moral judgment and societal expectations.

As I look back on my own history and past, I can witness (being gentle on myself) those times when my own defense of ego caused me to make great sacrifices to who I was—times when I didn't speak up when I knew I should have and times when I didn't defend myself or others, despite an inner knowing that I needed to. These reflections hold significant lessons; some come with increased wisdom and some with regrets. Either way, however, the experiences have taught me that I can stand proud in my values and successfully work through the fear. The stories below demonstrate the frequency and depth of threats to our self-esteem and the fear that results.

Meet Morgan:

I am the CEO of a medium-sized company. As I think about my work fears, so much of it for me is about the fear of being taken advantage of, being seen as a pushover, or not being valued and respected for my knowledge and expertise. I often wonder if I am making the right choices and decisions for my company and my employees. Fear can lead me to doubt my decisions. It causes me to question. Am I doing this right or not? Am I accepted as a leader? Am I valued, and are my skills valued? Am I seen as effective, and am I am making the right decision?

What I find is when I sit around the table, everyone is operating from some level of fear—fear of loss, fear of missed opportunity, fear of failure or success. I have to try and figure out what they fear. What are they most worried about? What are they really afraid of? Often, I am not just afraid that I will not come out ahead; I am afraid to come out behind. If I can rid myself of that fear, then I can get something done.

As you deal with fear in your organization and with your teams, establish trust right away, and then you can work on something together. With me, people know that we are going to learn from experiences; they are not going to be punished. When they know this, then it is very safe to come forth with thoughts, ideas, or concerns. When you have trust, I don't think you are afraid of what they will do. Employees' fear of repercussions is not there. The payoff is that they can take risks and know that they are not going to get terminated immediately if something goes wrong.

Morgan's story seeks to provide clarity not only in terms of how our fears around threats to our ego surface but also how leaders manage those threats in a healthy way. These examples show the challenges fear presents to us as leaders as well as how our workplace fears shape our decision making and leadership. She expressed distinct fears that reflected threats to her self-esteem. Her personal reflection brought forth a curiosity that promoted learning. This element of reflection promoted her ability to remain true to herself despite her fears. The ability to be self-aware of her fears effectively supported her to grow as a leader and aided her ability to develop her team.

In addition, there was recognition that entering relationships with this leadership style can take more time and energy. From an organizational perspective, as the senior leader for the company, Morgan assumed responsibility for creating a culture of safety and learning. She recognized that she acts as a role model in all her actions, and she takes that commitment very seriously. She demonstrated respect for each person's experiences of fear. She consciously developed environments of trust in her relationships. Morgan was not only able to assume ownership for her own fears, but she also understood the role she played in contributing to the fears of those around her.

Meet Geneva:

> I am a front-line leader. When I think of the occasions when I get fearful in my work, they generally center on whether I am good enough. I have this internal voice always questioning, "Do I have enough information? Am I going to do a good job? Will I meet everyone's expectations and demonstrate value?"
>
> When I set high standards, there's a little bit of fear about whether I can meet those standards. I have to remind myself that I don't always have all the answers, but I am an expert. I do have all that I need to be successful.
>
> The fear continues to go back to not looking good or not being perceived as a person who can do the job. There was one occasion during an executive session where I was going through the action plan to check the status of various items. Someone's ego kicked in. They started drilling me with questions that were over my head, and I had no answers. In my mind, I should have known the answer. I was left feeling incompetent. My fear was that I was being perceived as not knowing what I was talking about. I was afraid everyone would question why I was in the role and believe that I shouldn't be there.

I get so frustrated with myself after those experiences. Since I was in fear, my performance was not as strong as it could have been. I was left feeling helpless and stupid. I always have to change that perspective and tell myself that I'm not those things. I am very capable. Once I have boosted my confidence, I perform much better. The dynamics of fear actually made me minimize my own accomplishments.

Geneva expressed a perspective that reflects common employee and leader fears. In the workplace, our very survival is based on performing and demonstrating our expertise. We are judged and rated (generally annually in our review) based on how we have contributed, how good our work has been, and what value we have delivered to the organization. Our growth potential and perceived future opportunities are at risk and threatened when our ego and self-esteem is involved.

Fears stemming from threats to our confidence and competence can create shame and anger. When we (or our employees) can demonstrate awareness, we can mature from these fears and actually step into growth, as well as accountability. When we remain unaware and unconscious to the emotion of fear, we respond instinctually to these fears and generally demonstrate victim behaviors like blame, passive aggressive techniques, and avoidance. From an accountability perspective, these actions can be counterproductive to organizational goals. A critical role that leaders play is supporting employees (and themselves) to enhance their awareness and seek resources to support them in diminishing fear-based responses. Let's continue to explore additional examples of self-esteem threats and their impact.

Meet David:

> I operate in a senior leadership capacity at an academic institution. I am often afraid that I won't be respected for my level of contribution. When I work on team projects, I've had situations when coworkers step in and actually take the recognition and credit for work that was mine. All these things enhanced a feeling of fear. When I function as a team member, I wonder if people still see my contributions as a high-performing person without the others. There is not competitiveness necessarily, but I worry about being perceived as not being able to do things on my own. It's definitely about confidence. Once I feel confident about something, I am probably less afraid in the work environment.
>
> However, once I am in relationships of trust, it makes me more willing to share. I also find that once I have a proven expertise in a given area, my fear is minimized. In situations where the relationships are new or not as strong, I find myself feeling that I have to do things their way. The fear of judgment is heightened, and I can't always be my authentic self. My fear becomes, "Am I being who I truly am?"

David's story continues to bring the issue of power in our organizations to the surface. Threats to our ego can create a dynamic where we seek, or have a subconscious need, for more power and control. There is a belief that power will eliminate the threat. Sometimes, this is visible power. For example, this could be a formal position in the hierarchy like a managerial role. Other times, leaders and employees grasp for power by engaging in unethical behaviors or acts of betrayal. They might be deceitful or seek to make the mistakes of others public. They could fail to provide team members with necessary information. It is behavior we see frequently. Team members are aware of errors or allow a fellow coworker to make mistakes without correcting them, just waiting for that person to get caught or get in trouble.

As leaders, it's important for us to be aware of these behaviors in ourselves and our staff. If we desire a healthy, learning culture, we cannot tolerate these acts of direct or passive aggression from team members. It can be difficult not to encourage this behavior, particularly when we want to actively address performance issues. However, a more important goal is to establish an effective team. Performance will follow.

Triangulation of communication is another common symptom that can result from these fears. We can define triangulation of communication as situations where individuals involve a third party in their communication, thereby creating a triad or triangle. This can occur when one person shares or expresses an opinion or feeling on behalf of someone else. Triangulation of communication is one trap that leaders need to be cautious about, whether you use it yourself or you witness it on your team. This often inappropriately involves others and prevents us from engaging in more productive direct communication. We witness this in situations where one employee might complain to another about a problem or issues with team members expecting that employee to get involved.

For example, you might have a department meeting, and after the meeting, one employee comes to your office and shares that another employee was upset by a certain topic. Additionally, perhaps a team member comes to you, as the leader, sharing concerns about a fellow employee. In these situations, we often want to fix the problem, but it can be more effective to coach your employees to address the issue or facilitate discussions between them in an effort to resolve potential conflicts. While it may be tempting to entertain these types of discussions, as it allows you to know what the team is thinking, it actually undermines your team development. Additionally, it rewards the other employee with power that is undeserved. If you have a safe, effective team, the employee should feel safe to come to you directly. Establishing team guidelines or expectations can prevent these types of behaviors. It is also critical that as leaders we don't engage, encourage, or reward this behavior.

Below, George continues to share some of the struggles of leadership and how fears to our self-esteem can impact outcomes.

Meet George:

What am I afraid of at work? That is a loaded question. Having been fired from a job, you would think that it would be job loss. Interestingly, when I was fired, I was not so much worried about my financial security but my ego. It really hit my ego. I felt worthless, and I lacked confidence. In my situation, I was fired when my staff all went to my board of directors sharing deep concerns about me as a leader. As I look back, they were right to be concerned. I was not a good leader to them.

I didn't know how to lead. I was horrible. As many of us do, I had learned to lead from my manager. He used intimidation techniques and threats. Looking back, I feel so ashamed of how I treated people. I know how much a supervisor influences a person's experience in the workplace and in life, and I am sure I caused a great deal of pain to my staff.

At the time, I tried to justify my behavior. I was working in a very driven company and was under a great deal of stress and pressure to achieve certain goals. I felt so much fear in this regard. I was always on guard and put up barriers to protect myself. At some level, I knew I wasn't leading in an ideal way, but I didn't really know any other way. I had significant internal confusion about how best to lead.

As I looked back and reflected on that experience, I found myself exploring how I wanted to lead differently. This fear led me to make significant changes in my life. I became much more reflective. The biggest change I made in my leadership was to move from fear and intimidation to vision and alignment of people.

George's story demonstrates a great deal of vulnerability and regret. It speaks to the very nature of fears to our self-esteem but also demonstrates how we can move from those fears using awareness and reflection. How can we ever grow if we don't get clear about our mistakes? I believe strongly that we must be cautious about regret, and when we look back, we must often do so forgivingly of others and ourselves.

However, without this reflection, we cannot develop our own leadership. We can't improve and get better. I know I am not the same leader now that I was even five years ago. I hope none of us are. Development comes from this awareness of what we wish we had done differently—not harshly judging our mistakes, but learning from where we have been. The beauty is that we can continue to strengthen our abilities and make changes. We can embrace those moments of knowing and realize that we have another chance to get it right and do it better.

Meet Victoria:

I was a director—sort of a mid-level manager. My background was very different than many of my colleagues, and I was much younger (at the time) than most of the other leaders I worked with. I felt from day one that I was never on an equal playing field. I felt like I had to work a lot harder in a number of areas to be able to prove myself.

I felt like I was always on the defense, trying to justify my decisions and demonstrate my worth and value. There was this sense that, even though I knew I was qualified, no one else did. I didn't want anyone to have preconceived ideas that I might not be competent. I didn't hold the same level of education as many of the others I worked with, so I'm sure that contributed to my fear.

To me, I believed that my success was at risk. Without the respect of others, I feared I could not accomplish what I needed to in order to be successful. That comes back to my fear around competency. I was always defending my credibility. I found myself in a number of very confrontational situations where I had to defend my credibility, my qualifications, and myself.

In fear, I worry that I will lose something. Those losses could be projects that are important to me or the loss of a lot of hard work, but in the end, I cannot lose myself. That's all I have, and I can't allow fear to take that from me. I think the most difficult part is that I sometimes did things that went against my very nature just to achieve work objectives and get something done. I began to discover that I didn't necessarily like the person I was becoming. Ultimately, I found that the organization and the people I worked with valued something entirely different than what I valued.

While Victoria's story shows us how threats to our confidence and competency can create a strong defensive reaction, I think more importantly are her statements that, in those moments of defense, she risked losing herself. This is an important area of exploration. Under threat, we will always seek a strategy to save ourselves—fight or flight. This can look like a defensive strategy or a protection strategy. The question is not whether you will engage but rather how you will engage. As we think about the need to protect and defend, we have several options. First, we can change our perception of the threat. Awareness and reflection can allow us to assess the threat and the severity of threat. We might reach the conclusion that our fear is unsubstantiated, and therefore, we move into a different emotional experience all together.

However, if we continue to deem the situation to be a threat to our goal of preserving our self-esteem, confidence, and ego, then we will move into our second choice—how do we wish to respond? This is the critical next move and often makes or breaks our ability to stay true to ourselves. We (and our employees) always have a choice in how we manage a situation. Sometimes we act before giving ourselves an opportunity to really determine the best way to advance. When your competency is questioned in front of a large group of people, will you choose to yell and scream, or will you address the issue with the correct parties after the meeting? If a coworker just undermined your credibility, will you seek revenge, or will you have a crucial conversation with them about the inappropriateness of their behavior? There are always a hundred and one ways to address these types of issues—issues that surface frequently in our work lives and in our teams. How do you handle these situations as a leader?

How do you manage these situations with your staff? What do you allow, and how do you support your people?

Our very integrity is often on the line. The choices we make in these moments speak to our values, our character, and our authenticity. Can you be genuine and true to yourself? Under what circumstances do your struggle to maintain who you are? Where is your authenticity at risk of being compromised? How do you really want to lead?

Fear can result from our own insecurities and can be activated in response to others. It can surface as we process our internal baggage and work through our personal needs, and it can be linked to relationships with those around us and can reflect self-doubt—doubt around making the right choices or pursing the correct course of action, doubts about the intentions and assumptions of others, and doubts about our own resources and strength.

Many of the stories shared reflect feelings of, "Am I competent to be doing the work? Do I have the right skills and abilities? Am I valued? Am I recognized? Am I advancing? Do I have growth opportunities? Am I respected? Am I contributing? Or am I achieving my goals and the company goals?"

We fear the shame of failure, and we fear the risk of success. We fear staying in the old, and we fear moving to the new. When we consider fears that touch our ego, we experience a vulnerability that can either stifle or propel our growth. Situations of conflict and uncertainty elevate our self-esteem fears as we seek to find a place of equilibrium.

In earlier chapters, we discussed the role appraisal plays in emotion. As we think about fear and, more specifically, what we are afraid of, the notion of perception versus reality plays a critical role. If we believe, as I have asserted, that fear results from the perception of a threatening situation, and we believe that emotion is guided by our assessment of the situation— then it becomes critical that we accurately assess our current circumstances. Maybe, just maybe, we shouldn't be feeling fear, but rather we should be experiencing another emotion. This assessment of our emotional state can be critical as we seek to enhance self-awareness and get clear about what is really occurring in us.

Activity

Take a moment to consider your entire career. Using a long paper (or several pages combined), create a timeline of your career—a storyboard, so to speak. Add critical dates such as when you began certain jobs, went to school, graduated, achieved certifications, or left positions. You might even consider adding important dates from your personal life—marriages, children, deaths, or other significant life events. Consider the circumstances that were occurring around all of these events. Make note (in various colors, perhaps) of when you experienced threats to your self-esteem in these various situations.

The insights from this activity can be amazing. Consider the following questions:

What trends do you see when looking at your timeline?

_____

_____

_____

What typical reactions do you have to fear? Do you escape, do you fight, or do you compromise?

_____

_____

_____

What circumstances exist that lead you to experience self-esteem fears?

_____

_____

_____

When in your career have you lacked confidence? When have you risked not being yourself?

_____

_____

_____

When have you minimized your own accomplishments?

_____

_____

_____

What other emotions did you feel in these situations? Anger? Shame? Embarrassment? Sadness?

_____

_____

_____

What are your critical takeaways?

_____

_____

_____

OUR RESPONSE IN FEAR:
FIGHT OR FLIGHT

As we think about fear, psychology will tell us we have two general reactions: fight or flight[20]. In the workplace, this continues to be true, but the two perspectives take a different appearance. In the wild, we respond to fearful events in a somewhat simplistic way. I've watched National Geographic, and I've seen how this works. A heard of gazelle are grazing on the plains, minding their own business, tending to their young, and enjoying the warmth of the sun. Suddenly, they are startled by crackling branches. They begin to stampede through the grasses, stirring up a massive dust cloud behind them. Before you know it, the camera predictably spans to the three lionesses running feverishly, chasing them from behind. They zig and zag, lose their footing for a moment, regain it, and the hunt continues. How it ends is not relevant here (I always hate that part anyway), but the flight response was instinctual and a rapid reaction to threat.

Occasionally, however, you get the privilege of seeing the animals fight their predators. They typically find support in one another; they kick and exchange blows, pull the herd together, and gang up against the enemy. After winning the battle, we see the requirement to retain our survival is ingrained; it is innate. Have you seen an animal respond in any other way? Have you ever seen them give up? Have you ever seen them resign themselves to the fight? They don't act in those ways. The need to persevere is so strong that we engage in the battle. Sometimes we win; sometimes we lose, but we have fought nevertheless.

In our world, winning the fight isn't just about our physical survival; it's about the survival of our being. It's about protecting and securing the deepest part of who we are. Sometimes we run, sometimes we hide, and sometimes we fight. More often than not, others do the same. We are all in fear at some level, and we are all defending ourselves in some way. The question becomes, What are we fearful of, and what are we protecting ourselves from? When do we lay down the arms and realize that the threat may not be as severe as we initially thought, and when do we respond in more assertive ways?

As I think about this metaphor, I see people who will chase the heard and pick off the weakest player. I see the rest of the heard turn and run, leaving that person to die alone. I see teams that fight for one another and change entire cultures. I see people go into protection mode and hide under the rock until the threat has subsided. I see others who get clear about who they are and yell at the top of their lungs at the bear that drove them into the woods. Who are you in these metaphors? Are you running? Are you standing up? Are you the threatening lion, seeking the weak? Are you a small member of the heard standing up for the rest? It sounds easy when we think about it in these terms, but we also know that different situations require us to respond in various ways. When do you act in certain ways? What situations will you fight, and when will you seek refuge?

Our workplaces do not have to be an episode of *Wild Kingdom*. We don't have to raise the threat level to red. We can behave in ways that allow us to be true to ourselves and achieve outcomes. Understanding how we operate in fear can help us to do just that. In our workplaces, when we feel threatened in any of the ways described above, we will go into fight-or-flight mode, seeking to defend and protect ourselves.

Let's take a moment to better understand what types of behaviors we will engage in during fight or flight. What does it look like for us in the world of work? As we explore the narratives below, remember that situations, people, levels of trust, perceived support, and our experience all influence how we manage fear in various situations and what responses and coping mechanism we will assume. We can engage in fear-based situations in a healthy way or an unhealthy way. For example, revenge is a very real fight tactic, but it does not usually promote healthy workplace resolution. How do you react in fear? What responses to do you turn to?

Coping with Fear

In situations of fear, individuals will respond in a variety of ways as they seek defense and protection. Many of these defense mechanisms were originally advanced by Sigmund Freud and reflect an individual's protective reaction to perceptions of threat [21]. The examples below offer insight into how individuals will cope with fear and stress. None of the examples below are good or bad in their own right. They merely reflect ways that we cope. We use these methods to provide us with protection, yet often times the way we use them can actually exacerbate the situation we are in, thereby making it worse (or at least not as beneficial for us personally or for the team we work with).

While some might consider these defense mechanisms to be immature or low level responses, it seems reasonable to expect that fear as a primal emotion will result in basic coping responses. As we explore the strategies to address to fear, we will begin to learn options for coping with fear in a more conscious, advanced way.

The important consideration in assessing these coping mechanisms is to remember that we all access these strategies at some point in our emotional experience. Sometimes these strategies serve us, and sometimes they will keep us locked into our unpleasant situation. The assessment and awareness of our coping strategy will allow us to determine which of them will best support us in moving through fear. Assessing the effectiveness of a given strategy is the key. We also might find that one strategy is helpful for the individual but problematic for the leader or team. Some strategies support you in moving from fear; others will keep you locked into your emotion. Some, if used in healthy way, can be helpful, and others damaging.

As you read them, you will likely find yourself nodding your head in agreement. You might see yourself or your staff in these examples. Most of these are examples I have collected through my own research. While they do not necessarily fall in line with theoretical psychological definitions, I think they serve as strong examples which offer you the ability to relate and better understand how we react to fear.

As you read through them, consider how you react to fearful situations. How do your employees react? Are there certain circumstances where you might respond in one way and other experiences where you might act completely different?

Coping Mechanism #1: Avoidance/Denial

Many individuals will go into avoidance or denial when they are confronted with fear. They might deliberately or even unknowingly avoid certain people or situations that induce fear.

Kevin was part of a large work team and was feeling like his contribution to the project was a failure. He didn't see that he was adding value and was fearful that others believed the same. He stated:

> When I was stuck in fear, I beat myself up and avoided the situation. I believed someone else could just do it. It didn't have to be me. I didn't have the confidence to trust my efforts and my work, so I often avoided taking on stretch

assignments or additional projects for fear I
might not succeed.

For Kevin, there is a perception that he is safe from
fear and threat when he moves into denial and avoidance.
For leadership, this becomes a detriment when our
employees don't step up and bring all their strengths
and talents to their work. As an organization, we lose
creativity, innovation, and productivity when employees
suffer from fears that prevent them from assuming
responsibilities that empower themselves and the team.
What we really seek is to create environments where
high-performing employees feel safe and confident to
assume expanded roles and responsibilities.

Karen also found herself using denial to cope with
her experience of fear. Despite the fact that her boss was
having conversations with her about her performance,
she found herself denying the severity of her situation.
She stated:

> My manager was desperately trying to tell me
> something, and I just could not hear it. My
> performance was not up to par, and my denial
> prevented me from adjusting my actions in order
> to keep my job. It's easier to see that now. At
> the time, I felt fearful and angry, and I blamed
> everyone but myself.

A key function of our roles as leaders is to enhance
human performance. When people are in fear, they
might misunderstand or not hear the message we are

delivering. Again, they do this out of an instinctual need to protect themselves. Without the coping ability to deal with the problem, Karen was better off, in her mind, to assume the problem didn't exist.

Dealing with performance issues is perhaps one of the most difficult and fear-inducing aspects of a leader's job, both from the perspective of the leader and the employee. If we can't move employees from denial into acceptance of the issue, performance will not change. Our role as leaders is to not only break down their barriers so they can hear the message, but also provide the necessary support to aid them in moving out of fear. Our next chapter will provide these strategies.

Coping Mechanism #2: Rescue Me

Another common reaction in fear is that we wait for others to rescue us. There is a belief that clearly other people see what is happening here, and they will eventually help and come to the rescue. Surely they will not allow this situation to continue. When we are in fear, we feel as if we have no control of our circumstances. Waiting for others to help can contribute to this helpless feeling.

Jennifer was in a situation where she perceived she was being targeted by her boss. She shared:

> I thought other people have to see this and other people have to experience this type of behavior from this person, but nobody ever did. So it was kind of my hidden little secret. I kept hoping

someone would notice and rescue me, but they never did.

The "rescue me" syndrome can also occur amongst coworkers who all find themselves in a similar position. If we are all experiencing the same level of fear as a result of the same situation, we will seek support and strength from others. For individuals, this can be a healthy reaction to fear and can often minimize the personal feelings of isolation. When a significant number of employees share the same perspective, they can collectively turn this into personal power.

They might seek assistance from leadership at a higher level in the organization or turn to outside organizations for support (even considering unions as a support mechanism). While important for the individual employee, this can have negative implications for leaders and the organization. It is my opinion that leaders ideally maintain safe environments for employees to have open, honest discussion. When we stifle this with fear, we risk the implications that might not be ideal for us or the company we represent.

Coping Mechanism #3: Shutdown/Silence

Silence is another common response to fear. If being visible and speaking up results in danger, then the natural reaction to avoid the threat is to hide and remain quiet. As Don stated:

I managed the fear. I would keep to myself, just trying to hide and do my job as unnoticed as I could. In meetings, I would keep my opinions to myself. It didn't feel like it mattered much anyway.

When employees get to the point where they are reverting to silence, you often see other passive-aggressive behaviors that accompany the silence. They may begin to actively work to hide their mistakes or tell lies to prevent themselves from experiencing perceived negative consequences.

As we consider this from the broader perspective, leaders will often interpret silence for agreement. This is an erroneous assumption on their part and can have devastating consequences. When our employees are silent, we fail to hear everyone's perspective. We may lose out on great thoughts and opinions, and we certainly lose perspective on what the key issues are with the team. As employees shut down, they begin to become disengaged from their work, and performance suffers.

Coping Mechanism #4: Displacement

When individuals use displacement as a coping mechanism, they typically take their frustrations out on others, thereby displacing the emotion of fear, anger, or shame from themselves and moving it onto someone else. Displacement, therefore, becomes the action of transferring an emotion[22]. Fear is often accompanied by emotions of anger, embarrassment, shame, or guilt[23].

When we shift our emotions in the workplace, we might transfer our own fear and its complementary emotions unto others—be it our boss, coworkers, or subordinates. We might also take these emotions home, and our families suffer as well.

Dawn shared:

> As a leader of a small team, I had one individual who was struggling with his performance. We had several conversations about what he needed to change in order to be more successful in his role. I always had to carefully choose the time when I spoke to him, because he would get angry or frustrated, and then the rest of the team paid the price.

Tim had a similar comment:

> As an employee, I often found myself using this strategy. When I thought I was being criticized, it didn't feel like I could argue and share my perspective, so I often found myself getting angry with those around me for no reason or even giving them the silent treatment and not speaking to anyone. It felt like the only way to deal with it. I didn't know what else to do.

As a leader, Taylor found herself actually transferring her own fear-based behaviors to her team.

I felt so fearful but couldn't do anything about it. I almost just passed the fear right down the line. I would tell my staff that I have no choice. I am punished if our performance does not meet targets, so I punish them as well. Looking back (hindsight is twenty/twenty), I would have stopped the fear at me, managed the expectations differently, and led my staff to be successful. I would have supported them better to meet the goals and not passed down my own fear.

When individuals use displacement, we encounter a couple of potential problems. The first is we will often lack self-awareness or ownership of the role we assume in the problem. When we or our employees don't take accountability, nothing changes. The second problem is that when the behaviors continue, the team is penalized. Then morale of the entire group suffers.

Coping Mechanism #5: Aggressive Behavior

Aggressive behavior reflects our defense mechanism of fight. It typically surfaces when our fear backs us into a corner, and we perceive we have no way out. These behaviors show up in a variety of ways from acts of physical aggression to seeking formal and legal means of addressing the threat. Anger and frustration are complementary emotions to fear. Managers, coworkers, and work-related situations can create the perception of threat, and it can range from feeling that your safety is at risk (job loss) to your credibility.

Gabriel shared:

> My aggressive behaviors are in your face—raised voices and not letting the other person talk. I have had a number of very confrontational situations in front of large groups of people. There are times when I have walked into a meeting and been put on the spot. I have to defend myself. I don't like myself in those situations. However, fear also leads me to stand up for myself when I need to. I just have to make sure I'm doing it correctly.

Gabriel's response to fear demonstrates two ends of the spectrum. At one end, is her justification of the need to defend and "stand up for herself" against perceived attacks and threats. On the other end, she has the realization that this method is not helpful in the situation, nor is it effective. In assessing her response, she is clearly feeling like she is in a defensive position and therefore responds with higher levels of aggression. However, I would argue at the core of this situation is the feeling that she needs to stand up for herself. During our coaching conversation, we spent time focusing on that issue and how she could better manage that need. Ultimately, she was feeling a lack of support from those around her. By shifting her strategy and engaging others to support her work prior to entering meetings, she was able to eliminate the threat all together and hence her reaction to it.

What we often find when we consider our response to fear is that we are addressing and managing the wrong issue. We respond to the surface threat and often react from the primal emotion of fear, which creates the defense response. However, upon further assessment, we discover the core issue is a threat to self. When we delve into the real problem, we can actually generate more effective solutions. It reminds me of the metaphor of swimming in shark-infested waters. We can spend our energy trying to defend ourselves against the sharks, or we can consider how to swim in safer water or perhaps not enter the water at all.

Often, when our employees feel they are in position where they are not able to protect themselves, they will lash out with anger and threats. As leaders, when we can alter this perception, we shift the entire response that results. Stacy's example below demonstrates how this scenario can play out and what consequences can result. Stacy stated:

> When I feel like anyone is being attacked, instead of trying to go to safety, I will fight back. What I also know is that when managers become aggressive or get intimidating, people shut down, and we don't get anything done. I have also had occasions where I felt falsely accused by my boss. My job was on the line, and I had to go over his head. I went to human resources and had conversations with his boss.

When we, as leaders, create or subconsciously allow, environments of threat to exist, we assume great risk. People will defend themselves in very predicable ways. Conflict resolution can require significant effort and is time consuming and energy draining. As leaders, it is always more effective to manage employee and human resource issues at the department level. When employees feel the need to go to superiors and/or human resources, it signifies a breakdown in communication between the leader and employee. In defense of the leader, however, it can also signify a lack of accountability on the part of the employee. Managing these situations is challenging and often situation dependent.

For both employees and leaders, I always encourage the use of human resources. In most organizations, they are a valuable resource available to support both parties. For employees, they are an advocate and confidant, but only after you have assumed your own responsibility for the situation. For leaders, when you are working with challenging employees (and we always do), I encourage you to keep your leader and human resources involved and informed. If you are truly leading from a place of safety and respect, you have nothing to worry about. If not, then it is the right move for your employee to seek support from those above you.

In closing, acts of aggression in the workplace are often discouraged, but it never ceases to amaze me how frequently they occur. These types of behaviors tend to be fueled by intense emotions and can have devastating consequences, even legal action and claims of hostile work environments. My main point of caution for employees is to understand that this method of coping is rarely as successful as other strategies. There are more effective ways to manage these difficult situations which result in a better outcome for you, as an individual, and for the team. For organizations and leaders, the cautionary message is that allowing cultures of fear often results in behaviors of aggression which, in turn, can result in significant negative consequences including employment lawsuits, workplace violence, allegations of hostile work environment, increased turnover of high quality staff and decreased productivity.

Coping Mechanism #6: Surrender/Obedience/Resolute Compliance

At first glance, this might appear to be exactly what we want. We want obedience. We want people to do what they are asked, to do their job and not ask questions. Right? Wrong.

Mark shares:

> It's terrible. It's a horrible thing. I was afraid of retaliation, so I just complied. My manager told me not to argue or I would regret it. If I disagreed and said anything, I would be disciplined, so I just did the work—even when I knew I was doing it wrong. I just did what was I was told. At some point, I had to give in just to survive. After the first quarter, the numbers came out,

and our team errors and injuries had increased while performance had dropped off significantly. I know it's wrong, but I felt happy—a sense of vindication or something. The company allowed it to continue for two more quarters, and then my supervisor was fired. As I look back, I wish I would have handled it differently, but at the time, I felt like I had no choice.

When we lead from fear, we may be able to get people to comply, but they will not feel good about it. They will never be committed to the team, the work, or the organization. Performance will suffer, and outcomes will drop. Looking at these key indicators is often a marker of whether fear exists in your work team or company. When our performance declines, a fair question to pose is, What is the level of fear in the organization?

Perhaps you have answered this question with a resounding, "*High*—the level of fear in my company is very high." Now what? The first item to consider is where the fear is coming from. Is it organization wide or just your department? Is it coming from your leader or all leadership? If you are a leader, are you part of the problem or are you trying to be the solution?

Some of you might feel like you are being led by fear from those above you. In assessing your own position, we have discussed the challenges leaders face as they navigate managing their own fears and the fears of others. The first step is always to begin to gain control of your own emotions of fear. If you operate in a fear based culture, you need to consider your position of influence and how you want to lead up in a different way. Explore the steps you can take to not advance the fear in the culture. What difficult conversations do you need to have with others? What boundaries do you need to create for yourself? As you read the book, you are absorbing the information with two lenses; one as an employee and the other as a leader. Be true to yourself above all.

Therefore, in addition to managing our own personal fears, you also have a responsibility to minimize this fear for your people. This makes our role very important. We must get clear on the fear we are experiencing ourselves and begin to manage our own reaction and response to it. If we can't control our fear, then we have very little chance of helping others navigate theirs. If we, as individuals are experiencing fear, it is generally safe to say that we are using fear as a tactic with others. If you are seeing your performance indicators fall short of targets, consider how you are leading. Are you using fear with others? It is important to be honest with this assessment as we begin to explore alternative strategies for leading without fear.

Coping Mechanism #7: Passive-Aggressive Behavior

Passive-aggressive behavior allows us to indirectly express our emotions of fear and anger. As leaders, they can be hard to recognize and even more difficult to address. They show up in the rumor mill, in unscrupulous tactics, through the use of sarcasm, and even sabotage.

Casey stated:

> I was angry, hurt, and scared. I felt like I needed to protect myself, and I wanted to sabotage my coworkers—almost make them pay for what they were doing to me.

Carry used deceptive behavior as her means of protection. She expressed:

> I did not want to go and ask questions, because I felt like if I asked a question, it was a sign of weakness. I was afraid of what the answer would be, or I was afraid that my boss would think I should know the answer and question my competency. So I began to get a bit deceptive. I would hide mistakes, blame others, and cover my tail. I even did this when I didn't need to. It became such a habit.

As leaders, we deal with employees who use passive-aggressive techniques. We hear stories from other employees, and we have a sense that something is going on. We often feel like we have to catch people in the act in order to have the conversation, but I would encourage you to not wait. While these behaviors can be difficult to get your arms around, they can be some of the most destructive methods of coping. They can compromise personal integrity and the integrity of the team. Consider whether you engage in any of these behaviors. Consider whether your staff is using this as a coping mechanism.

If you see these behaviors occurring in your staff, it is best to revisit the accountability model; establishing expectations, seek mutual commitment and hold others responsible. Have you successfully established behavioral expectations for your team which discussed these passive aggressive behaviors and their negative consequences? Have you achieved mutual commitment from your team members to these expectations? Are you holding people responsible?

There are a couple of pitfalls worth noting. The very nature of passive-aggressive behavior makes it difficult to identify, observe, and act upon. In addition to creating expectations around these specific behaviors, also develop expectations around how employees should respond to team mates who are engaging in these behaviors. Employees often do not know how to react when they see teammates acting and using passive aggressive techniques. Helping them to problem solve how to manage their colleagues can be critical.

Another pitfall can be managing passive-aggressive employees through the team. It is often tempting to want to address these behaviors in a team meeting, hoping that the employee who is utilizing these techniques will get the message through osmosis. The best way to manage these behaviors as a leader is to address the employee one on one through a very direct conversation. In this conversation, spend time outlining the specific behavior you or others witnessed, what you see as the negative impact of that behavior to the team, and what you expect that employee to do differently. This can be a method for engaging in the discussion. Another tip in these conversations is to lead with powerful questions. The more you can coach the employee to see the impact of their actions, the better. The following statements and questions are helpful:

- I am observing (insert behavior). Tell me what is occurring for you when you engage in those behaviors.
- What do you see from your teammates when you act that way?
- What are you trying to accomplish? What is your goal?
- How could you respond differently (better) and still achieve your desired outcomes. With this question, you might have to assist them with brainstorming. Often, individuals who use passive aggressive techniques have learned to be successful and do not know any other way.

I would like to make one final important point as you engage in this conversation. Establishing ground rules at the beginning of the conversation can be an important step as a leader to ensure that the employee does not take the conversation off course. Examples might be:

- Keep the discussion focused on the employee and what is within their control. This prevents them from bringing others into the discussion (e.g. "Catherine is just as frustrated as I am" or "John does the same thing"). For this conversation, you are focused on that employee and only their behavior.

- Define that you do not want to see blaming, accusations or other behaviors surface in your discussion.
- Explain that you want the discussion to be productive and that will require the two of you to focus on the specific issues and not be distracted by other topics. If others surface, make note of them and come back to them in a later conversation.

As we noted, passive-aggressive behaviors can destroy team motivation and success. Addressing these behaviors immediately and in a non-threatening way is critical. It is also important for leaders to ensure they are not engaging in passive aggressive behaviors. Too often, leaders will ask other employees to watch their fellow employees and report back on their behavior or they will blame others for their own leadership shortcoming. These are destructive to team cohesion and can have negative results. Continue to be aware of your own risks and vulnerabilities in these situations. Consider how you can address it.

Coping Mechanism #8: Projection

When in fear, we might find ourselves projecting our behaviors unto others with very little awareness that we are even doing it. From a pure psychological perspective, projection occurs when an individual takes characteristics or motives that they themselves possess and attributes those to others [24]. When we use this concept more loosely, we find situations when we or others are unaware of our own motives and reflect those unto others. When we use terms such as, "that's the pot calling the kettle black" or "they need to hold the mirror up to themselves," we might be referring to individuals who are projecting without any knowledge of their actions.

Darrin explained:

> I was working with a team recently and found myself a victim of projection. I had recently gone through a restructure of our department. I had a new boss who was promoted from within and knew me well. As she was beginning to have conversations with other teams across the company, one of our senior leaders shared feedback with her about my poor follow-through. As it turned out, the senior leader was actually projecting his issues onto me. It was actually he that was struggling with follow-through problems. If my new boss didn't know me, she might have believed that feedback about me. That would have generated fear in me, and who knows what my response would have been.

Projection can occur in various ways. Sometimes leaders can project onto their employees, or sometimes coworkers might project onto each other. As leaders, we seek to ensure we are delivering real and honest feedback in order to improve performance. If we remain unaware of projection issues, we will not be addressing the correct problem with the right individual. Projection occurs very unconsciously, and unless we seek self-awareness and knowledge, we remain stuck in this blind spot. Therefore, it is important that we also remain vigilant and critical of feedback we receive about employees in order to prevent fear that might result from projection errors.

Coping Mechanism #9: Employees Give Up

Everything you do and everything you say as a leader impacts others. We too frequently jump to discipline as our only mechanism of holding others accountable. When we silence the voice of our employees and move so rapidly to punishment, we begin to gain compliance (sometimes)—but at what cost? Employees reach the point where they will do what they are told and only what they are told. They fail to look for more effective ways to manage a problem. The organization fails to have employees recognize and address more systematic issues. The greater risk is the organization fails in moving forward.

Trevor had tremendous strength in problem solving. He was a master at identifying an issue in his area and knowing how to fix it.

I just naturally see where things could be done better. I would recognize when people were too involved in their box and when we could look at issues differently and work together to make all our jobs easier. My manager would tell me to just do my job and mind my own business. I would put a lot of effort into proving myself, and it was exhausting, so I just gave up. The problem was there were many things falling through the cracks. We were all so busy doing our own work, we didn't see where we were duplicating efforts or even stepping on each other and canceling out each other's work.

The more disengaged our employees become, the more at risk we are of declining performance. At some point, people don't just give up, but they engage in the passive-aggressive behaviors discussed above. Ultimately, however, we don't just squelch great ideas and passion; we impact the team and the organization's ability to be more successful in their work.

Coping Mechanism #10: Rationalization

When we begin to rationalize, we attempt to explain unacceptable behaviors in a rational and intellectual way. We might try to avoid the emotion all together and only see the goal through the eyes of our logical side. While it is often important to bring in our cognitive assessment, we can never clear the emotion from the event, nor would we want to. In fact, our emotion can actually be a strength to our rationalization. [25]

Where we can get into trouble is when we get so lost in the rationalization that we fail to see or address the real issue. We might fail to protect and defend ourselves appropriately when we seek to abolish the emotional element. We have spoken frequently of behaviors we see in the workplace. They might be verbally or physically aggressive or even circumstances that diminish our credibility.

If we try to rationalize it, we might say, "I'm sure he didn't mean it. I probably misunderstood. This individual is under a lot of pressure and stress right now. That's not how they typically react. Maybe that's not what they meant to say or do." While these might be very accurate statements in terms of someone's behavior, if we are not careful, we can actually rationalize very inappropriate behavior. We frequently see this with victims of abuse. They find a very logical reason to justify what they are experiencing. If we engage in rationalization to frequently, we continue to validate behaviors that are not acceptable. In these circumstances, we can begin to minimize its impact of various negative actions upon us and lose our awareness for how destructive they actually are.

Sometimes, rationalization is a wonderful, effective strategy. It makes sense and perhaps we did overreact. There are circumstances when individuals are under a great deal of stress and they react in less than ideal ways. These are situations which we can overlook and rationalize in a way that is healthy for us and the other person.

However, in situations of threat, we make these statements all the time. You might make these justifications about your boss's behavior or a coworker's behavior, and your employees are likely making these same excuses. Think about how you might rationalize when you feel threatened. This is the key point to note when assessing whether rationalization is a healthy coping strategy for you or not. If you are rationalizing behavior where you actually felt threatened, consider this a trigger. Aggressive behaviors in which we might rationalize in a healthy way usually do not feel threatening. It may feel like venting or a display of anger, but we won't feel threatened by it. If you repeatedly feel threatened or engage in behaviors where others feel threatened, consider this a red flag.

In summary, rationalization can be a very effective coping mechanism. Other times, it can keep us trapped in denial about the severity of the issue we are experiencing. If we are not careful with rationalization, it can prevent us from recognizing a legitimate threat. As a leader, consider whether you feed your employees with rational statements in an effort to prevent them from feeling the fear—fear which you may have intended to use in the moment but perhaps regret now, fear which you might feel no control over, or fear which you are trying to stop.

Coping Mechanism #11: Regression

Regression can often link with aspects of aggression or passive-aggressive behaviors. When we are experiencing situations where we can't or do not know how to cope, we might revert to earlier stages of development[26]. We might find ourselves (or our staff) pouting when we hear bad news or throwing a temper tantrum. We might engage in deceptive behavior, similar to how we acted as a child when we sought to get our siblings in trouble.

Regression can be a sign for leaders. When circumstances exceed our capacity to cope, we might revert to regression. As a leader, witnessing these behaviors in yourself or others can be a sign that employees are overwhelmed and not able to manage their emotional experience on their own. They need help and support. They need you to engage in the strategies outlined in the next chapter.

Coping Mechanism #12: Staying Stuck

Michelle shares an excellent example of what it looks and feels like to be stuck in fear. She expressed:

> *Stuck* is probably a good word. It keeps me very comfortable. In some ways, comfort is great, and in some ways, comfort is boring. I actually have a situation right now where I have been in my position for five years. I am bored to tears. I am ready to take on something new. There are some openings in another division, and I am very

interested in one of them. I don't know what to do. I have talked with my close friends and colleagues about it, but for some reason, I feel stuck. So right now, I am paralyzed by fear. I have tried to drop hints to people who might have influence. It's ridiculous. I am an educated person with a high level of authority, and I can't even go directly to this person. I need to increase my confidence. As I think about this, my fear is not allowing me to move forward. I am very comfortable in my position. I am good at my position, and I'm scared to take a risk, so I just stay.

This is a typical and very frequently reported feeling when individuals are in fear. From a leader's perspective, we are often promoting our high performers and encouraging them to take on additional assignments, assume more risk, and even pursue opportunities for higher-level positions in the company. We talent map employees and conduct succession planning with the hope that our strong employees will advance and grow. It's important to realize that when employees are in a place of fear and feel a lack of confidence about their skill set to move forward, they will remain in their comfortable situation.

I recently had the privilege of working with a very strong leader. Her skills and leadership had developed rapidly over a years' time frame as she sought various development opportunities. She was ready for an advanced role and had begun to pursue other career opportunities. The problem came when she was offered another job—an incredible promotion. Employers were extending her amazing offers, and she was paralyzed and fearful to accept them, worried that she wouldn't be good enough to be successful.

This is the place where leaders have to be sure to engage in strategies that boost confidence. They must create support structures to ease the anxiety and make employees feel safe and comfortable in pursuing advanced opportunities. As we consider the dynamics of fear, we have to help employees fill in the gaps and recognize their own strengths in order to ease self-concerns about their own capabilities. This is where leadership gets exciting and fun. These are the places we live for as we help others tap into their own sense of power and confidence.

As individuals, we need to consider these same questions. How can we take ownership of our own career growth? It requires us to break down the barriers of fear and begin to increase our own confidence level about what is possible for us. We must also seek support to help us navigate potentially new waters.

Coping Mechanism #13: Switching the Goal

I once heard a statement that resonates with me to this day. It indicated that when we are confronted with a situation or problem, we always have three choices. First, we can accept the situation. Second, we can change the situation. Last, we can change our perception of the situation. It's a revision of the serenity prayer: "God, grant me the serenity to accept the things I cannot change; the courage to change the things I can; and wisdom to know the difference."

As we consider our experiences in fear, these three choices ring true. The challenge becomes knowing which of the three options is best to pursue in any given situation. This differentiation can often make or break the situations we find ourselves in. As a coach, this is often why clients seek out my services.

The first step in this process is to get clear on what is your true goal. This part, in and of itself, can be difficult, because it means we have to get honest with ourselves in a way that we are not always accustomed (I will introduce this concept here, but we will discuss this further in later chapters). Is your goal to keep your job? Do you want to be respected? Do you need to feel more a part of the group? Or, deep down, are you wanting someone else to look bad, be seen as the hero for the team, or do you just want to have a voice in your work. Our goals can encompass a host of perspectives, but the more clarity we can achieve with what are goals are, the more likely we are to know which path to take. Knowing what we want from our circumstances is critical in allowing us to move through the fear.

There are others question we can pose as we consider our goals and our desired outcome. Do our goals assume positive intent? Do they serve the greater good? Is the outcome we are seeing what we want to see? How important is the situation to you? Asking these questions assists us in achieving clarity as to the goal.

This then serves as the foundation to which of the three options you should pursue; accept the situation, change the situation or change your perception of the situation.

Let's discuss each option individually. Our first option is that we can accept the situation. As with any coping strategy, this can serve us and improve our circumstances or hinder us. As with the serenity prayer, we often must accept the things we cannot change. Below is a quick checklist to assist in determining those things that are often worth just accepting:

- Is the outcome or situation unimportant to you? All too often, we become fearful or frustrated by events that really don't even matter to us. These are easy items to accept and let go of.
- Is the outcome or situation outside of your control? If you truly have no control of the situation, than being fearful of it is not serving you. Accept the situation and move on.
- Are there aspects of the situation that are within your control? Sometimes, there are parts of the situation that are within our control. In those cases, it might make sense to consider changing those aspects of the situation. One item worthy of note here is that we always have control of whether we stay or leave in a given situation. This brings me to my final question.
- Is this truly a situation that you can accept? This is the most important question to consider as you decide whether to accept the situation or pursue one of the other two alternatives. One tell

sign of whether we can truly be in acceptance or not is whether we continue to complain, vent or feel strong emotions (fear, anger etc) about the situation. If you do, then likely you need to change the situation or change your perception of it.

The second option, change the situation, really gets to the heart of our ability to assume control of our situation. We can consider the same questions from above as we determine whether this strategy is the desired and correct course of action. If the issue is important to us and we cannot just accept it, we must change the situation. If the circumstances are such that we cannot accept them, than we must change them. Throughout the book, we have discussed the need to take control of our situation if we are to reduce fear. Our ability to change the situation falls along a very long continuum with countless options within it. If you deem that you must change the situation, go back to the beginning, get clear on your goals and then outline all the options available to you along that continuum. You might be able to change various aspects of the situation, you might have influence over certain areas or you might have to avoid or leave the situation.

In working with clients, this is a frequent exercise we engage in. There are times when individuals will exhaust their options to change and the last step is to leave. There were examples of that in the stories from above. Sometimes the greatest control we take over fear is to remove ourselves from the situations that create it.

The third option, changing our perception of the situation, directly addresses the coping strategy of switching the goal. When we consider switching the goal, we are seeking to change our perception of the situation; we are seeking the wisdom to know the difference. Where we have to be cautious is be sure we know the difference. Often, this might serve us in better managing the situations we are in. I recently heard a wonderful example of how changing our perception of a situation can serve us. A leader was recently let go from a position and made the following comment, "this did not happen *to* me, it happened *for* me." Consider how this change in perception might impact this individual's ability to navigate a very difficult situation. Often, if we can change our perception of our circumstances, it can actively support us in dealing with fear and other challenges.

Other times, it can get in our way, stifling our growth and causing us to settle for something far less than we deserve or are capable of pursuing. We might say, "If I can't get my voice heard, then I will just be quiet. If I can't get that promotion, then I'll just stay here." The original goal is altered to something that feels more attainable. While this can feel like an excellent way to cope, it rarely serves us in feeling more fulfilled in our role, nor does it allow us to contribute in a way that brings forth our strengths. Often, it can leave us feeling resentful of our leaders and teammates. The trick to this strategy as a coping mechanism is to know when adjusting the goal is a positive step and when it is actually compromising our strength. We must ask ourselves, "When are we switching the goal as an effective coping strategy, and when is switching the goal hindering our potential?"

Coping Mechanism #14: Affiliation

When we are in fear, we seek support. We will look for others who can assist us, others who can protect us, and others who may have experienced what we are going through. We are looking for advice, structures to aid us in achieving our goals, and ways to make us feel more confident in our situation. We are looking for aspects of control and the ability to decrease the uncertainty of our situation.

As leaders, supporting people and providing for their needs is perhaps one of the greatest ways we can shift our employees out of fear. We support them when we give them stretch projects or assignments and ensure they have the resources they need to be successful. Support can also appear when we give them performance feedback and create structures that allow them to improve, or when they feel threatened and we ease their threat by communicating an honest message.

The Role of Coping

Keep in mind that none of the coping mechanisms above are good or bad. They exist and can have healing properties when used to support us effectively, or they can have negative implications, which keep us trapped in a cycle of fear. As you consider yourself or your staff, where do you go when in fear? What situations create a response of avoidance or aggression?

As I consider this question from a personal perspective, I can tell you I have gone into avoidance when the conflict is highly tenuous or escalated. When emotions and anger run high, I have to fight the urge to go into denial. When I don't have relationships with people and they come across arrogant, I have resorted to passive-aggressive behavior or resolute compliance— like a child who says, "You didn't tell me to pick up all the dishes, just the glasses."

I seek affiliation when I engage in a challenge and need support to get me through it. I also seek greater self-awareness to enable me to engage in more productive coping strategies for myself and for those I work with. If we are looking at our past and present with total honesty, we can likely find situations where we have successfully and unsuccessfully engaged in many of these coping strategies.

The coping strategies we choose depend on our situations. They depend on our values and personality. They are contingent upon our goals and motivations. Consider how you respond to various fears. When have you used the coping mechanisms outlined above? What do you see your staff doing? How do they react?

Impacting Factors for Fear

As we consider our ability to cope with fear and the reaction we might take in fear, we know that certain variables will impact our ability to successfully cope with fear (or not experience fear at all, but rather some complimentary, less severe emotion like challenge). Here is what we know about fear:

- When we can act and be confident about our situation or issue, we will experience less fear.
- When we feel supported by our leader, coworkers, family, and others around us, we will experience less fear.
- When we have experience navigating the same or similar event, we will experience less fear.
- When we have more real or perceived control over the situation, we have less fear.
- When we are more certain about the outcome of a situation, we will experience less fear.

As we look at leadership strategies in later chapters, they will focus on ways leaders can enhance these variables. Leaders play a significant role in helping people cope with their fears. They first have to create workplaces that minimize fear in order to generate safety and openness. The last chapter focuses on strategies to assist in doing just that. However, leaders must also provide support in helping people navigate their emotional experiences at work. We must coach and guide employees to choose proper, appropriate coping mechanisms and aid them in evaluating their options and seeking the best approach. Before we discuss the strategies, however, it is helpful to understand what fear looks and sounds like in our workplaces.

THE FIRE:
LEADERSHIP BEHAVIORS
THAT FUEL THE FLAME

The Language of Fear

We have a choice.

We always have a choice.

I recently attended a lecture on our capacity and potential as humans. We were asked to contemplate situations where we felt loss, failure, or missed opportunities to realize our potential. Wow, did that bring forward a laundry list of options! There were conversations I wished I would have had differently, times I wished I would have stood up for myself in a more assertive way, and opportunities that I just watched pass by me. I found myself thinking about all those occasions where I may have stayed silent instead of speaking my truth or acted out when I should have been quiet and listened.

The point of the exercise was not to generate regret but rather to realize that those opportunities still exist. The previous moments serve as learning tools, and we now have opportunities to continue to realize a new potential for ourselves and for those around us. As leaders, we serve as a conduit for growth and development. We have the ultimate pleasure (and, let's be honest, sometimes burden) of guiding a team of individuals to achieve their own personal potential—their own greatness.

As I consider the issues of fear, both from personal experience and from the countless stories I have been a part of, I am reminded of all the missed opportunities that exist when we operate from fear. There is a way in life that we expand and contract, build and collapse. When we are in fear, we contract and collapse onto ourselves. We can feel it in our bodies as we shrink from the person or situation. We are not able to respond from a place of strength. What we need to learn is that there is a way that we can move from our experiences of collapsing into fear and learn to use them to realize our potential.

Some of us went into leadership because of a sacred calling. There was a deep sense, a lifelong knowing that we would lead others. We were destined to serve in this capacity, and we seek to fulfill this calling every day in our work. Others of us were thrown into the fire. We were good at our work—someone saw something in us—and before we knew it, we were in a leadership role. Sometimes, we were given support in this new world; other times, it might have felt like learning to swim for the first time—as long as you could keep your head above water, you were still in the game.

I say these things to frame the conversation below. As we consider the language of fear, consider the words, as well as verbal and nonverbal behaviors, that instill fear—both in us and in our employees. I like to preface this section with empathy. Have empathy for yourself and empathy for those around you. Sometimes we are too hard on ourselves; sometimes we are not hard enough. I am writing this, believing that we all want to lead from a better place. We want to lead in ways that are not only more effective for the organization but healthier for the people we lead. Those individuals who trust us and look to us to help them through work want us to lead better. Work reflects an aspect of our lives that occupies more time and attention than other aspects of our lives. We have an obligation to our employees, our organizations, and ourselves to create environments where people thrive and expand—not contract and shrivel up.

Your honesty with the discussion below will serve you; it will enhance your awareness and allow you to be open to new and better ways to lead. Be open and honest with yourself, and allow yourself to explore and grow. Allow yourself to heal from your own mistakes, and allow yourself to realize a new potential.

What we hear can be threatening.

The pages that follow provide examples of language and behavior that can be fear based. They are in no particular order. This is intentional to keep you thinking in various directions. Below are a few examples (and just a few) of what fear-based language might sound like[27]:

- This cannot happen again, or someone will be fired. (Direct threats to our job security)
- Why are you doing it that way? That seems ridiculous. (Belittling statements)
- Why would you even think of doing it that way? (Imposing judgment and belittling)
- Anyone could have done that; even my kindergartner could have come up with a better plan (Condescending language, belittling)
- You just don't get it, do you? (Insults)
- You have three days to turn this around. Figure it out and get it done. (Threats and lack of support)
- You're not going to present that, are you? (Discounting work or ideas)
- We're going to raise the bar, and I'm worried that you're performance sucks and you're not good enough. (Intimidation, belittling)
- I need to have one head to shoot if this doesn't go right. (Verbally berated, violent language)
- You really shot yourself in the foot that time. We are going to war. (Violent, battle language.)
- All of your colleagues are complaining about your performance. (Bringing others into the discussion when they can't speak for themselves)
- Prove to me that you... (Requiring evidence of others)
- You are being insubordinate. (Threats)
- I am going to have to open up a formal investigation into your actions. (Threats)

- That's not what I'm paying you for. (Condescending language)
- Is that the best you could come up with? (Insulting, belittling)
- I don't like surprises. Don't ever let me enter a meeting and be surprised. (Threats)

Activity

The list below includes many actions, behaviors, and items that can lead to environments of fear or fear-based reactions. Review the list and carefully examine situations where you have experienced these behaviors from a leader and/or coworker in the workplace. Circle the items below that you have personally experienced. Make a quick note as to what occurred in the situation.

Chart 1

Raised voices, yelling or shouting	Not being given a key assignment	Criticized in front of others
Fists pounding on the table	Ineffective conflict	Rumors spread about me
Abruptness, short interactions	Inability to express your opinion	Someone failing to deny false rumors about me

Belitting comments, insults or put down's	Retaliation or perception of possible retaliation	Aggressive behaviors
Sarcastic comments	Put in my place	Discounting my ideas
Eye rolling	Undermining my efforts	Taking credit for my ideas
Sabotage of my work	Frequently cover your tracks	Use of profanity/ swearing
Glaring looks, wicked eye contact, dark stares	Showed me who was boss	Backstabbing
No eye contact	Withheld positive recognition	Hiding mistakes or errors
Silence/silent treatment	Given "crap" work or unwanted assignment	Angry waving of arms or fists
Passive aggressive behaviors (excluding you from key communication)	Intimidation tactics	Threats about your job

Ignoring me	Internal competition between employees or teams is promoted	Telling lies or hiding the truth
Outward attempts to make me look bad	High absenteeism or turnover	Physical/sexual threats (you'd better watch you back, I'll get you for that, this isn't over yet)
Verbally berated	Accusations against me	Throwing of objects
Verbally berated in front of others	Name calling	Unwillingness to take initiative or risks
Unfair performance evaluation	Offensive/ insulting comments	Unethical behaviors that you were asked to contribute to
Not given clear direction, held accountable to standards you were not aware of	Labeling me (either by race, sex, political affiliation etc.)	Refusal to provide necessary resources for you to do your job
Nitpicking my work	Being put on the spot	Blaming you
Intimidating/ Authoritative presence	Embarrassment/ humiliation (public or private)	Bring others into the issues (such and such said...)

Others override your thoughts	Punished for speaking up	Condescending language
Impose judgment	Play favorites	Send mixed messages
Shunning	People are suspicious–"Prove it to me"	Witnesses present for the discussion

The list seems to go on and on. It's difficult to imagine that all these behaviors can be fear inducing, yet these items are all a potential catalyst for fear. In isolation, they are not likely to generate a strong sense of fear, but a culture of these behaviors—a leader and team exhibiting these behaviors frequently—will induce fear in employees (and yourself as a leader). There is a response that occurs from the stimulus of fear.

> When we are afraid to speak up, we learn to be silent.

> When we are afraid of punishment, we learn to cover our mistakes.

> When we are afraid of knowing too much, we learn to withhold information.

> When were afraid of isolation, we learn to conform.

When we are afraid of change, we maintain the status quo.

When we are afraid of failure, we learn to stay in our comfort zone.

What are you afraid of? What reaction is it creating for you? What are your employees afraid of, and how is it impacting them?

Consider the list above. As you think about the behaviors and experiences you circled, consider what emotion that event generated for you. Was it fear? Anxiety? Anger? Something else? Use the space below to note your key insights.

_____

_____

_____

_____

Next, I want you to begin to get honest about your own leadership. When do you exhibit these behaviors with your employees or people you work with? Again, do not judge yourself. Don't consider whether your behavior is right or wrong or whether it is justified. Just be aware of your own behavior and note which of the behaviors you might engage in, either consciously or unconsciously. Which situations might trigger different reactions or responses? If you circled any of the items above, it's time to get serious. What are you experiencing? What is your staff experiencing? Use this list to engage your team in conversation.

Make a list of those areas where you find yourself using these tactics as a leader.

Chart 2

If we review the list above, perhaps you selected *withholding positive feedback*. Consider all the reasons why you might do this with your staff. As I talk with individuals, sometimes they feel like they have missed the opportunity in the moment to deliver feedback, and then too much time passes, and it seemed irrelevant. They may have also felt time constraints that prevented them from providing instantaneous feedback. Other leaders have gotten truly honest with themselves and shared that they sometimes withheld positive feedback because they felt threatened by the other individual, and their own esteem issues prevented them from recognizing another.

Consider the impact of this behavior from the employee's perspective. If we believe that positive reinforcement drives behavior change, we are actually acting counterproductive to our goals when we fail to recognize others. By providing positive feedback, we strengthen the desired behavior. In this case, our own issues as leaders get in the way of the greater goals. This is a perfect example of when fear is primal. Our own fear as leaders overrides any other rational action we might take.

Let's try another example: put people in their place. I have worked with numerous organizations that used an interesting tactic to get people to be present and on time for meetings. I actually found myself surprised by how often this approach is used. At some companies (many, as it turns out), once a meeting starts, the doors are locked, and no one else can enter. The strategy was implemented as a mechanism to encourage employees to be on time and avoid the disruption of people coming in late. While tardiness can be a genuine problem in organizations, what I found in talking with people is how belittling this tactic was for employees. It inadvertently created the perception of no respect and no trust. It sent a collective message to the group that they were not adults who could manage themselves effectively. Employees believed that a better option would be to communicate the importance of being on time, and if certain individuals were problematic, have the conversation directly with those people.

As a final example, let's explore passive-aggressive behaviors. In environments of fear, people are out for survival. It becomes a mentality where the last man standing wins the round. I worked with one group of individuals at a large retailer. They each had very high productivity targets for stocking shelves within their designated area. They were rated and incentivized by their ability to meet or exceed individual numbers.

When daily targets were not met, the ramifications were significant, and often people were fired for their inability to reach these daily goals. As punishments increased, teamwork declined. Everyone looked out for number one, even to the point of sabotaging others. Often there were occasions when one individual would have a higher workload one night and a lighter workload the next, yet the culture of fear generated behaviors where no one would assist each other. When staff did help one another, they had to hide it; otherwise the individual who was assisted was reprimanded. A second dynamic was that individuals always started in entry-level roles and had to work their way up. By throwing each other under the bus, making false accusations, and not supporting each other, there was a perceived ability to climb the ladder more rapidly.

I used to think these behaviors were extreme and isolated, but I have come to discover that they are highly prevalent. I used to find myself wondering how people could so easily compromise their integrity for a job, advancement, or to preserve their ego. Yet, as those of you who have experience in these environments can attest, you truly lose yourself in the culture. You lose yourself to the point where you often don't even see what you've done or who you have become. That is where the self-awareness becomes so critical. Take time to explore the list above and ask yourself the critical questions. Where am I in fear, and where do I exhibit these behaviors? Where is my staff at on the fear continuum? How do I begin to shift?

The Impact of Fear

As we started to explore with the examples above, when employees are in fear, they dread going to work. That can be one of the most telling signs. Whether they can consciously link their feeling of trepidation to specific fears is not as relevant as the mere fact that when employees don't want to come in, fear is likely to exist.

As individuals, when we are in fear, we limit our own capacity and remain stuck in situations that are not meeting our needs. We limit our own potential, and the impact can be health issues, family issues, and work issues.

As leaders, when employees are in fear, it shrinks or contracts their thinking. They are not able to be creative, they cannot be open, and they have no capacity or willingness to take productive risks. We limit our ability to motivate and get the best from our people when we lead from fear.

The ultimate cost at the organizational level is that fear generates behaviors that negatively affect satisfaction, performance, and success. We know that retention suffers, error rates often increase, and other outcomes falter[28].

Again, consider your own behaviors when you are in fear. Are you able to access your potential from that state? Are you operating at your best when fear surrounds you? Likely, your response is no, and if you are limited by fear, then so are your employees.

I often like to speak to Deming's fourteen-point quality program. For those familiar with Deming, he is considered a guru in achieving quality management. He outlines fourteen steps, which, if followed, will lead to increase quality, efficiency, and effectiveness. One of Deming's fourteen points is "drive out fear." Ultimately, the idea stems from the fact that if fear exists, it prevents employees from performing at their best. From a quality perspective, people need to feel secure and safe to bring thoughts, ideas, and concerns forward [29].

I was recently part of a meeting where about ten attendees from various parts of the organization were present. As various topics were discussed, the leader of the group was getting visibility agitated and eventually lashed out at two of the participants with frustration at not being kept in the loop. While generally this was a group with strong comradery, it was clear that this leader's behavior had caused everyone in the room to shut down and be silent. For the remainder of the meeting, he tried to recover and get people's voices into the room, but it was too late. When individuals are in fear, they will exhibit more risk-adverse behaviors in individual judgments, decision making, and choices. This was seen both in the meeting and the work the group produced following the meeting.

Can Fear Be a Motivator?

Motivation in the workplace has been studied from countless perspectives dating back to the classic Hawthorne studies which sought to determine the ideal work environment for maximizing performance. Since then, many other theories have surfaced which help to explain how employees are motivated at work. Researchers have explored various needs theories, goals orientation models and incentive systems. We have looked at carrot-and-stick approaches, which basically incorporate enticements or punishments. We have considered involvement, growth, and empowerment [30]. More recently, researchers have also begun to explore the role of positive emotions, such as happiness, pride and interest in motivation.

In American culture, in the workplace, and in many of our social systems (political, parenting), we have often come to believe that fear motivates behavior change. Many even assert that it is the key motivator. However, in all these venues, it actually has the opposite impact. When we lead from fear—whether it is with our employees, children, or social organizations—all we really achieve is immobilization. We reinforce the paralysis of employees and prevent them from using independent decision making or bringing forth creative ideas. There is just not space for these things to occur when an individual is in a state of fear. When in fear, we contract, minimize our own potential, lose creative and risk-taking ability, and are generally unmotivated. We need safety to be creative, security to take risks, courage to share ideas, and trust to be vulnerable. Fear has a counter effect.

There are a number of studies that look at the use of fear in political, health or other types of advertising campaigns [31]. Many of these studies show the effectiveness of such campaigns in generating a desired behavior change. Based in the premise of fear appeal theory, the overall assumption is that by sending a message that creates fear of significant negative consequences (i.e., death from smoking), one can motivate others to alleviate the fear by changing their behavior. If I change my action, I will feel less fear which is rewarding. The theory is complex, but the success of the fear appeal ultimately requires individuals to feel that they have the necessary resources to avoid the threat which is being specified[32]. In the workplace, we might say state that a threat of being fired would then result in employees doing what they are told in order to avoid the consequence of job loss.

The greatest differentiator in this discussion, however, is the desired outcome of the fear appeal. Do we just want employees to "do what they are told"? Do you want compliance or commitment? Obedience or creativity? Conformity or innovation? When we think about fear as a management practice that is consciously or unconsciously justified as a motivator, there are a few items worthy of consideration.

There are times when all we want is compliance and obedience. We create appeals that play to fear of death to make people act in healthier ways, fear of fire risk to encourage home safety, or fear of political ramifications to persuade individuals to vote a certain way. Research on fear appeals, like what is presented above, are conducted based on simple messages that we want people to obey. They do not involve complexity and do not require or even promote the need for critical or creative thinking.

The second factor is, not only are these appeals simple "orders," they are also accompanied by an individual's belief that they can cope with the situation or they have the resources to avoid the threat. If I am told in my work that I must achieve a certain level of production in order to keep my job, but I don't feel I have the resources, support or coping ability to achieve that target, no amount of fear will create success. It will actually cause me to withdraw and retreat. If fear results in the avoidance of threat, that is all individuals will seek to accomplish.

In the past decade, there has been a great deal of research around "positive psychology." As we have discussed, negative emotions, such as fear, leave individuals in a state of existence and mere survival. These negative emotions narrow our thinking whereas positive emotions have been found to broaden our cognition, creativity and innovation[33]. The real question than, as we think about fear as a motivator, is what situations are we using it in and what we do seek to accomplish?

In the workplace, our broader desire for employee engagement tends to be more intricate. We seek employees who are empowered, exhibit critical thinking and creativity. We want high levels of innovation and productivity. As we consider the use of fear as a motivator and the research findings in light of organizational motivation and behavior, there are two items worthy of discussion, which seem to be critical variables in situations where fear can result in desired behavior change.

- Key elements of the situation must be within a person's direct control[34].When this occurs, individuals have a greater ability to navigate their own situational elements.
- Support structures must be in place to guide correct decision making. The ultimate question we must answer yes to is, can I cope with my situation? [35]

When we consider our own experiences of fear and those occasions when fear sends us into paralysis versus a place of strength, what we often find (and what my research has told me) is when fear is self-induced, it can be more of a catapult or motivator than when fear is pushed upon us by others. A good example of this is when you accept a promotion or start a new job. There is usually fear around the unknown—whether you will be successful or how you will fit in. However, since this is a decision within your power and that you actually self selected, despite the level of fear, you can manage the event and the emotion that comes with it. Therefore, due to our control over the situation, we have the ability to gauge and monitor the fear in a way that serves us.

Additionally, what we have come to learn is that the purpose of fear is to alert us of potential dangers and place us into a heightened state of awareness—

awareness of risks, threats, and dangers. When fear is self-imposed, it can be useful in alerting us to when and how we might take calculated risks. It provides us with a preparedness that can be an asset when we are seeking growth opportunities. When we read books about how to embrace fear, make it your friend, use it to your advantage, or allow it to catapult you to greatness, we are often reading about levels of fear and components of situations that are within our control. When fear is self-induced, it can be a motivator, because we have more control of our circumstances.

What we also know from the research above regarding fear and behavior change is that when fear is accompanied by adequate levels of support, its negative impact can be minimized. If we consider aspects of fear from previous discussions, we have learned that fear is enhanced by greater uncertainty and perceived by lack of control over one's circumstances. Therefore, even in the presence of fear, if we as leaders can provide high levels of support, we can actually mitigate levels of fear. This is confirmed by data stating that role clarity, predictability with rules, and the empowerment of employees will actually decrease fear[36]. I don't think this necessarily supports an argument to use fear, but it can assist us in understanding how we can reduce fear in situations where fear might be beyond our control. Those instances where an honest message, regardless of how well it is communicated, will induce fear in employees. Providing strategic support for employees fills the gap between transparency and fear.

As we think about this in terms of motivational implications, sometimes leaders will argue that using fear deliberately as a motivator can have the desired impact. What appears to be the case, based on research, is that sometimes (and I emphasize *only sometimes*) in the short term, you might see the desired result by using fear, but fear cannot be a long-term motivator and will not result in long-term, consistent high performance. Ultimately, organizational cultures of fear lead to perceptions of failure, inadequacy, and retaliation[37].

If you hold a deep-seeded belief that fear is a positive motivator, then my arguments are not for you. I hold an equally opposite perspective, and my purpose is not to convince you, but rather to teach you why fear is not an effective approach and how to do it differently. My purpose is to help you understand fear and come to your own awareness, through your own experiences, as to why fear has not been successful for you. The key question when considering the deliberate use of fear is what you are trying to accomplish. Ultimately, you will not achieve broader, sustainable results by using fear. At best, you might get temporary compliance, but in the long run, you will begin to see highly destructive behaviors surface.

Activity

Consider times when you have experienced fear as a motivator. What were the circumstances? Did the two rules (self-induced and support) apply to your situations?

When has fear been a de-motivator for you? What were the implications for you and for your performance?

Knowing that at times we all use fear in an attempt to motivate, what were the situations when you found yourself resorting to fear? What circumstances drove you to use fear?

Why Leaders Resort to Fear

Throughout the interviews, and in some of the stories expressed throughout the book, leaders have admitted they use fear in an effort to achieve their goals. Perhaps they were even successful when they used fear and so that perception keeps them using it as a tactic for business practice. I have talked with leaders who stated, "I have turned to fear tactics as a way of managing unproductive behaviors and to get things done. I have used power plays to establish my own authority. I have instilled fear to keep people from pushing back."

Let's begin to break down some of the various, highly legitimate reasons we use fear in the workplace as a management tactic. I say legitimate because there are real reasons why leaders resort to fear. What I hope to establish is a sense of awareness around your own reasons for using fear.

I Need to Establish a Sense of Urgency with My Employees

One of the greatest reasons I hear for why leaders use fear is that they need to establish a sense of urgency around an issue or problem, and they can't find any other way to create the appropriate level of tension.

Richard stated:

> When I have a deep desire for a given outcome or I need people to understand how serious an issue is, I will often resort to fear tactics and engage in the behavior or language of fear. I might make threats or speak to employees inappropriately. As my level of passion increases, I'm sure I come across with an elevated voice and a harsh tone. Sometimes, I might even pit employees against each other in an effort to create competition or publically embarrass someone in an effort to light a fire underneath them. What I don't often realize in the moment is the negative impact this creates. Sometimes it takes a while to see it. Other times it surfaces immediately.

Similarly, leaders can often reach a point of desperation where the issue is so serious they don't know any other way.

Stacy states:

> I wanted to maintain a sense of control. I felt lost and hopeless, and I didn't know what else to do. I was feeling so pressured that I wanted my employees to feel that same level of stress that I was under. I would inappropriately put them on the spot; I would judge their ideas. I wouldn't

allow them to contribute. I probably even played favorites.

I Don't Know Any Other Way

As we consider fear, the need for action and accountability is an underlying variable. Often, we perceive the need for control and believe that somehow we can shame, anger, and scare people into behavior change. As we enter this place of desperation, there is an ongoing sense leaders express that they just don't know what else to do. They feel exhausted by their own fight and lost in what to do next. I don't know any other way.

Because our culture is inundated with fear and fear-based tactics from the time we are children, we learn these methods. Often, we don't learn any other tools, or this method has become so comfortable that we maintain it in light of others options that might be more effective.

I Am Engulfed in the Flames of My Own Fear

The final, most common reason I find for why leaders use fear is that they are in fear. We use fear because we are afraid. The activities up to this point were designed to assist you in identifying areas where you are experiencing fear yourself. It is extremely difficult to not lead from fear when we are suffocating in fear. It requires extreme discipline, and one might even argue that it is impossible. When we are in fear, we will almost always project that onto others.

When I work with teams and see cultures of fear, I always start with assessing the fear level of leadership. If there is fear in the organizational culture or amongst teams of employees, 99 percent of the time, I find there is fear in the leader.

Jayson shared:

> For me personally, the most difficult aspect of fear to explore was the ego-based fears. I recently had a situation where I took over a project from another team. There was a great deal of cross collaboration between multiple teams, so the moving parts were significant. I had about twelve highly competent people working on the project, and I felt good about the team, at least on the surface. What I came to realize was much different. I was so scared of getting it wrong. It was high profile work, and I felt like it was all occurring outside my control. Everyone was doing their own thing, and I felt left out of the loop.
>
> During one meeting, I lost it. I yelled at the group, shared my frustration, and pulled everything in. All assignments, work steps, everything needed to come through me. I took a highly functioning, empowered team and crushed them. My ego got in my own way, and my fears around the success of the project

took over. I also quickly overwhelmed myself with tasks and was not able to keep up. No one stepped up, since I had just stripped them of their power. They just sat back and waited for direction. It was terrible. Worse yet, it was my own fault. It had a devastating impact to my relationships with these individuals and unfortunately impacted other projects that I needed to work with them on.

When leaders are in fear, be it their own security, sense of affiliation, or self-esteem fears, they become blind to how they might be using fear in their own leadership. As Jayson displayed, leaders often use fear tactics to protect their own egos. This is probably the most difficult place to explore. Our self-esteem and ego are in place to protect us, and achieving awareness around fears in this area can be challenging. As we consider why we use fear, know that your own fears are always worth understanding. It is from our fears that we find ourselves using fear with others.

As we've stated before, what we really seek is a culture of accountability. Most of the time, leaders don't want to instill fear; they really desire employees to own their work and the results of the team. If what we are really trying to do is establish a sense of urgency and a culture of accountability, then let's do that. Let's accomplish that through healthy leadership approaches and strategies and not through the use of fear. The following chapters will begin to outline strategies that support a more effective method of achieving this goal.

A Model of Fear in the Workplace

Let's begin to break down all these different variables and concepts, putting them together into a model of fear[38].

Model of Fear

1. Goal: All emotion begins as a reaction to whether an event supports or hinders a goal. We ask ourselves whether any given event supports or hinders our personal well being.

2. Appraisal of threat: At this point, we move into an appraisal of the event—seeking to assess the nature of the event in relation to our goal. Any time we perceive an event as a threat, we will move into fear.

3. Impacting factors for appraisal: In conjunction with the appraisal of threat, fear brings with it a perception of little control over individual circumstances, a sense of uncertainty about the outcome, and the belief that others are to blame for the situation. By changing these variables, we will naturally shift the emotion from one of fear to some other emotion (i.e., challenge). As we consider strategies, we will assess ways to increase control, decrease uncertainty, and shift fault and blame in a way to move individuals from fear.

4. Factors impacting fear: In addition to the factors above, fear is also impacted by an individual's confidence in managing a situation, the support they are provided to navigate the fearful event, and any experience they bring from dealing with similar situations in the past. Again, these three variables provide a foundation for strategies leaders can use as they move employees out of fear.

5. Fear is the reaction and emotion we move into when we experience a threat to our safety, security, affiliation, belonging, or self-esteem and ego.

6. Reaction to fear: when we are in fear, we respond through protection and defense, which often surfaces as a fight-or-flight response. As we discussed above, reactions can range from avoidance to aggression. These reactions and coping mechanisms will often keep us stuck in our present circumstances. Until we address the variables that impact fear, we cannot move into increased self-awareness, reflection, learning, and adaptation. Once we successfully move into these spaces, we can take our staff and ourselves out of fear.

Moving out of fear is the true objective, but how do we accomplish that goal? The strategies below begin to outline how we eliminate fear from our workplaces and move our teams and ourselves from fear.

Activity

Let's begin to explore the elements of fear from the model above. Consider a current leadership challenge you are experiencing. Is there a project or outcome in your area that is not proceeding as expected? Do you have a situation where you are not achieving the desired result? Perhaps it is a project or initiative you are leading? Maybe it's a specific situation with an employee? Often there are elements of fear at work in those situations where we are struggling.

- In the example that you selected, what is your goal? What is it that you are really trying to accomplish? Identify all your goals, not just those on the surface. What are your business goals? What are your personal goals? What are your affiliation and ego goals?

  _____

  _____

- What threats are you experiencing in this situation? What threats are those you work with on this issue experiencing? How are those threats the same or different? Again, consider all the threats from security to affiliation to self-esteem threats.

  _____

  _____

- Let's take a look at the factors impacting appraisal. Given your example, where do you feel a lack of control? Where do others feel little control? How can you bring more control to the situation for both yourself and your employees or team members?

  _____

- There are also factors impacting the threat. Where is your level of confidence with the work? How are you being supported? How are you supporting others? What additional support would help you and your team through this situation?

- Finally, let's look at how you and others are coping. What response are you exhibiting? Are you withdrawing or shutting down? Are others getting aggressive? How are these responses serving you? How are they preventing you from moving from fear?

We've spent this chapter exploring the language of fear, the impact of fear, and why leaders use fear. Allow these lessons to provide you with warnings of when fear might be permeating your work environment. When you find yourself or others displaying fear-based language or behavior, let the red flag go up. Know that you are entering situations or creating environments that are fear based, and you must proactively address them for your personal health, the health of your employees, and the success of the organization.

CONTROLLING THE BURN:
LEADERSHIP STRATEGIES FOR REDUCING FEAR IN THE WORKPLACE

Tips for Reducing Fear in the Workplace

Often in writing on leadership and fear there is a disciplinary tone, lecturing leaders on the negative impact of fear—trying to convince you of all the horrible things that happen when leaders use fear in the workplace. More importantly than chastising leaders for engaging in fear-based behaviors, I hope to teach what causes fear, people's reactions to fear, and what fear looks and sounds like in the workplace.

Like most leaders, I speak from the voice of an employee and the voice of a leader. I speak from the voice of someone who has experienced fear and someone who has likely induced fear. I speak my voice and that of those around me who have shared their personal stories.

As leaders, we have a message to deliver. We have an honest organizational reality that we must address. Establishing accountability requires us to deliver an authentic message without the appraisal of fear by our employees. Because fear narrows thinking[39], the way we communicate that message and the environment we create becomes critical. One of the challenges we experience as leaders, and what we've learned from our work thus far, is that we can deliver the same message to fifteen employees, and based upon their goals and personal judgments, they will all interpret that message differently and experience different emotions based on the message. That leaves you with an incredible challenge.

When we begin to implement and communicate an organizational reality, it is important to consider the various emotional responses that an event might generate. For example, what if our organization was going to be restructuring the division? That simple message could be interpreted as a threat by many employees (perhaps even all employees). If employees have previously had bad experiences with restructures, they might assume there will be layoffs and be fearful. Other employees might reserve judgment until further information comes out, while others might immediately begin searching for other roles, not willing or able to manage the ambiguity.

The key role of leaders is to create and implement the organizational strategies and deliver the organizational messages in a way that promotes productive goal achievement by our employees. We must deliver these messages in a way that encourages accountability. In the end, we want our employees to be successful so that our team and the organization can be successful. We want to meet our goals, reach our potential, and thrive in our work environments. What we also know (hopefully) is that fear actually diminishes our capacity to do these things. Therefore, what we hope to do is decrease the level of fear in our work environments as we deliver and implement an organizational reality.

Reducing Fear in the Organization

The graphic above can assist us in understanding this concept, and the strategies that follow will support you in reducing fear. If we can deliver messages, those honest organizational realities, and execute strategies using the tips below, we can change the emotional experience for our employees and thereby reduce fear. We can even begin to use what might have been fear in a way that energizes employees and motivates them to explore and conquer challenges in a healthy, productive way.

As leaders, we have the ability to lead differently. Despite our organizational cultures, our team dynamics, or our own leaders, we can make a choice to lead another way. We can change cultures by shifting our own behavior and thus our team's behavior. Additionally, as individual employees, we can influence change. We don't have to remain stuck in fear. We can reclaim our power and take back our control. By doing so, we recover our losses; we reclaim ourselves. When in fear, we tend to justify the abnormal as normal. We begin to think the situation we are in is acceptable—it's right, it's okay. The strategies that follow will aid you in becoming aware of your fears and the role fear is playing in your work environment, and they will provide techniques for mitigating fear.

Strategy 1: Increase Self-Awareness

Self-awareness is an ongoing practice. It is essentially our ability to know ourselves, our motives, desires, personality—who we are and why we do what we do. It is only with self-awareness that we grow and learn. Many researchers, theorists, and spiritual traditions embrace and practice this strategy as a first step to all other knowing. With self-awareness, we develop the capacity to be consciously aware of our values and motives—our actions and reactions. We develop introspection. We find time and energy to pay attention to signals our bodies are sending us. We focus on the thoughts in our minds and the actions we are taking that support or run counter to our purposes.

Self-awareness is not a one-time activity that you complete and finish. It's not a book that you purchase and study, or even a class that you take. It is a lifestyle that you adopt—an ongoing practice you engage in. Having self-awareness requires regular introspection. This can take the form of formal practices such as journaling or mediation, or less formal avenues through the allocation of thought time to just be aware. It is often those moments of clarity where we realize why we feel the way we do or we see something in ourselves that we have never noticed.

The activities that have preceded this chapter were rooted in attempting to increase your personal self-awareness, but they cannot be a single action. As you have completed all the activities in this book, what have you discovered about those things that are important to you? What did you learn about your reaction to fear and the role of fear in your work life? Your takeaways today will look different tomorrow. Your situations will be different. Your challenges will be altered. You will grow and change, and your awareness must change with that learning.

In relation to the elements of emotion, we know from previous chapters what is important to us. These variables impact who we are at the core and what we value. They represent key drivers of emotions. It is with self-awareness that we gain clarity around these elements and about our goals. We begin to understand when they are working for us and when they need to be altered. Awareness helps us to determine whether our appraisals are accurate and what aspects of the situation we need to actively alter in order to better meet our needs. Being self-aware is about getting clear, and with this clarity comes an increased understanding of ourselves, others, and the environment we operate within.

Self-awareness begins with an open mind. It requires us to be compassionate, attentive, and non-judgmental—primarily of ourselves. The same defenses that we create for others, we also instill in ourselves, and these mechanisms can be a block for our own awareness.

I deliver countless personality assessments and debrief sessions every year. I use multiple instruments, all of which are statistically valid and reliable. It never fails, however, that I hear individuals, upon receiving their results, say, "This is wrong. This doesn't fit me at all. I'm not like that. I don't do those things." We all have blind spots, and our minds work hard to protect us from what we might not be able to admit.

When we are in situations and can create a heightened sense of self-awareness, we can witness our circumstances from a new perspective. We can look at it through the eyes of a video camera and slow down the events in a way that helps us to notice and seek insight.

We can become exposed to emerging opportunities and a shift in experience.

As we consider this in relation to fear, think about your responses to the exercises that have preceded this chapter. What have you discovered about your own fears? What did you learn about the way you might use fear with others? Where do you experience or use fear-based behaviors? Where are you surrounded by real fear? Where do you merely have false perceptions of fear? What are you threatened by? What are your goals? How are you appraising the situation? While the list of questions seems daunting, continuously exploring these issues supports insight into yourself that aids in transformation.

Activity: What Are You Afraid Of?

Part of increasing self-awareness is getting control of your own fear, and until you do, you will not be able to lead from any other place. As we've discussed, we often lead from fear when we ourselves are in a place of fear.

A common practice that many psychologists and leadership coaches use is a simple exercise. Find a friend or confidant—you might even look for a stranger. Sit face to face for a minimum of five minutes. Have this person ask you the simple question, "What are you afraid of?" Engage in no other discussion. The other person is only to ask that simple question after each of your statements for the time allotted. Go deep, get clear, and be honest. Rotate with your partner after five minutes, and allow them to respond to the question as you ask it: "What are you afraid of?"

What were your key insights?

What did you notice?

When I first conducted this activity, I heard statements such as: I'm afraid of tornadoes, spiders, closed spaced, etc.

Keep digging.

As time passed, I then began to hear: I'm afraid of loneliness, rejection, not fitting in, being fired.

Keep going.

Then I hear: I'm afraid of losing myself to this company that doesn't value me. I'm afraid I am becoming someone else. I'm afraid I will permanently damage others trying to succeed. I'm afraid I've given up and can't go back.

This is where the truth lies. This is where we discover the insights that will change your life.

Be aware of how you are using fear and how you might be instilling fear in others Are you using fear to manipulate? Are you using fear to create urgency? How else might you engage in fear-based behaviors? Be bold, ask tough questions, push boundaries, and test the limits. Additionally, recognize your own power. Be aware of the power you hold over yourself and others. Recognize the power you have in all your situations and circumstances, and own that power.

Finally, address your own fears first. With self-awareness, you can understand your emotions. Until you can manage your own fears, you cannot assist others in dealing with theirs, and you will likely not be able to lead in any other way. Follow the steps below in relation to yourself before you apply them to others. Release your own ego defenses. Let go of the arrogance that protects you and realize that you're not any better or any worse than anyone else. Get curious about who you are, what you want, and how you live and lead. Release judgment, let go of fear, and imagine how you can be different in those spaces. Be conscious of your leadership choices for yourself and others. Until you are aware, you cannot make change. Self-awareness is the foundation of all else to come and the basis of behavior change.

Strategy 2: Be Clear on All Your Goals and Adjust Them to Serve You

All emotions are driven from congruence or opposition to our goals. If we experience a positive emotion, it tells us that we are on track in achieving our goals. If I want a raise in my salary and get one, I am happy. A positive emotion tells me I am moving forward toward personal goal achievement. When we experience a negative emotion, something is amiss—not quite right. When we are angry or fearful in a situation, it is a signal that the situation we are in is not supporting our ultimate goal.

In partnership with self-awareness, we must be clear on our goals. Only then will we know when something is threatening them. In the workplace, is your goal to keep your job, look good, build a strong team of capable people, or ensure you are "in good" with the boss? Is it having others look to you for the answers? Do you need to hold power? Is your goal to do quality work with few errors, be a mentor for your employees, or provide an environment where they can shine? Do you need to have ample time with your family? Do you seek work and life balance? All of these examples guide our ultimate path and provide the foundation for our emotional experience.

What are your goals? What are your team's goals? The company's goals? Are they aligned? When we think about fear resulting from threat, and more importantly, when we consider the notion of accountability and organizational commitment, it is critical that we have goal alignment. If your personal goals are significantly different than the company goals, you will likely experience a different level of threat as a result. When we are out of alignment with others in terms of goals, we feel torn, dissatisfied, and fearful.

Activity

What are your personal goals? Consider not only hard, tangible goals, but your soft goals as well.

_____

_____

What are your larger goals, and what are your smaller, situational goals?

_____

_____

What are you seeking to accomplish in any given moment during any interaction?

_____

_____

What are you seeking from the experience of work?

_____

_____

What do you need from work in order to support your personal or family needs?

_____

_____

What are your team/company goals, and how aligned are they?

_____

_____

Additionally, as a leader, you need to consider these questions from the perspective of your employees, or you need to assist your employees in considering these items themselves. How will you get clarity on these questions in relation to your staff?

_____

_____

Evaluate the Goal

Knowing your goals is the first step. Understanding their impact is the second. As we consider our goals, we have to get clear on how they are serving us in a positive way and when they might be preventing us from achieving what we need. Sometimes our goals can be counterproductive. For example, I might want to keep my job and have a significant amount of power. My behaviors as I seek power might actually be preventing me from being successful in my job and thus placing my job at risk.

When we think about the goal in relation to fear, it is also important to consider whether the goal is actually serving our greater good. Perhaps our primary goal is to look good and show competence in front of a decision-making group. In the process of doing so, we might then engage in highly unproductive behaviors with fellow team members. We might think that for us to look good, others must look bad, and therefore we withhold information, "forget" to invite key players to the meeting, or sabotage the efforts of those we work with. We might actually be engaging in fear-based behaviors in order to achieve these objectives at the expense of greater organizational performance. In the short term, we might see this as acceptable. Ultimately, however, we only compromise our ability to meet larger organizational needs. The old saying what comes around goes around can hold truth in these circumstances.

While assessing our goals can reveal negative patterns such as those above, it can also expose less dramatic incongruencies. Often we have to consider shifting the goal in order to achieve higher levels of productivity and stronger outcomes. When we look at cause and effect, it might be important to shed some goals so other purposes can emerge. For example, we may need to spend valuable meeting time discussing the softer stuff instead of always focusing on process and goal status. Perhaps we let go of winning and being right in order to support the consideration of other ideas. While your end goal might be increased financial performance, an intermediate goal could be increased employee engagement. Teambuilding and open, honest discussion might be required to achieve that objective.

As we discussed earlier in the book, all the events and situations in our lives, particularly those that generate a negative emotional experience, benefit from assessment of our goals and what we want from a particular situation. It is this assessment of our needs that aids us in understanding how our actions and subsequent emotions are surfacing. When in fear, we have goals that are threatened. Until we get clear on where the threat is coming from and what exactly is being threatened, we are not in a position to alter the experience of fear.

I recently had an experience with a client that created deep frustration. This individual was struggling at work. She had recently taken on significant additional responsibilities in her leadership role and was not seeing the results she desired. Her project team was failing, and she was exhibiting fear for both her job and her credibility. There was one project in particular with high visibility that surfaced as an example. She had a team of seven individuals who were highly competent, capable, and independent. They had been working autonomously on this issue before she assumed leadership, and they were moving forward despite the role she now had over them. They were all highly self-directed, strong in their skills, and very experienced in their roles and the work of the group.

At first, this seemed to be the perfect group to lead. However, as we explored her goals, we discovered a deep need for her to be seen as the primary driver of the project. She wanted to be in charge. When she began to honestly explore her true needs, she found that she wanted credit for the group's efforts and believed she needed more control of their assignments. She also needed to be seen as an integral part of the work. In reality, she needed to not only be an integral part of the work; she wanted to own the work. There were places where she believed the group was off track, and she needed them to get back on board. Those goals drove her behavior from the beginning.

As a result of those goals, she took more control of the efforts, required direct supervision and approval of every aspect of the project, and verbally reprimanded team members who did not follow this protocol. This reaction caused all of the employees, who were originally highly engaged and very strong in their project efforts, to pull back. They waited for direction, became passive aggressive, and their work on the project declined severely. The project went off track and off schedule. While she originally sought credit for the excellent work of this team, she now wanted to distance herself. She was leading from a place of fear and projecting her fears onto them through her leadership.

As we explored her frustration, we realized that she was deeply protecting her self-esteem and ego to the point where she was driving away all her new teammates. Her actual goals created a counter effect to what she desired. Through continued discussion of her goals, her honest assessment of what she really wanted surfaced and provided insight into how to shift the goals (and her perspective) in order to better serve her. What she realized is the goal she really desired was a successful project completion. In seeking to control the group, her behavior was negatively impacting the team and preventing them from achieving that goal. By focusing on a different goal, she was able to redirect the work efforts and change her own behavior in a way to support the project's success. Her shift was from needing to own the project with the goal of taking credit for the work, to supporting a high-functioning team and sharing credit for a project well executed.

As another example, I recently worked with a leader who decided to go back to school to pursue her master's degree. She was struggling to balance the demands of work, family, and school. In order to be successful, she had dropped out of an activity she enjoyed (painting) and discontinued her exercise routine. She felt like she was abandoning her family and didn't have the time and energy she desired. As we explored her goals, she was desperately seeking to give 150 percent to all of the things she used to do, particularly her family. In her mind, the only way she could incorporate school was to drop other activities.

As we continued to delve into the issue, what she came to realize is that she could shift some of her goals and still maintain the balance she ultimately desired. There is a concept in physics called leverage. It refers to the need to exert the least amount of effort to achieve the greatest result. This is a critical way that we conserve energy. As she thought about this concept in relation to her goals, she realized that she could achieve her school goals of learning and getting good grades by using leverage. She was able to determine areas where she was exerting more effort than needed and not achieving an increased outcome. One example was with her presentations. She would spend a great deal of time positioning the graphs perfectly on the page and continuing changing the colors of her graphs. Often, this would take hours for her to complete and did not make the final product better. She also found ways that she could leverage both school and family goals by studing with her kids and maximizing their time as a family.

Reevaluating our goals and determining when to adjust them is a critical first step in managing our emotions and the emotion of fear. I like to advise people to consider being unattached to the outcome. There are some goals and outcomes that require attachment. Keeping your job might be one of them. However, as much as possible, try detaching yourself from a specific outcome. Be open to what might emerge. When we hold on less tightly, we are less likely to be disappointed by the result and therefore less likely to experience a negative emotion. (I think there is a song around this concept.)

Consider those times when you have a really great idea. Your goal is to sell your idea and get everyone bought into it. When people don't buy in, you feel angry, frustrated, and disappointed. What if your goal was to share your idea and solicit input from others? When you shift the goal, you shift the emotion. No matter what people say, you are open and receiving.

Think of an issue you have at work that you are problem solving. As you are considering and evaluating the possible options, this is the time to seek input. Ask some of your peers or employees what they think are reasonable alternatives. Share your thoughts and solicit theirs. Now, incorporating their input, craft the final recommendation. We all too often seek buy in after we are sold on our own idea. At that point, our goal then becomes to force this solution onto others. If we shift the goal, we are less frustrated by the result.

Activity

When you are experiencing fear or other emotions, consider your goal. What is it?

_____

_____

Is that goal serving your greater good?

_____

_____

Could you alter it in a way that still leads to a desired positive outcome but shifts your emotional experience?

_____

_____

Is there a way you could become less attached to the outcome?

_____

_____

How might you use this strategy in those areas where you are feeling fear or other negative emotions?

A few years ago, I worked with a team who needed to restructure their division. Leadership was taking a bold step and asking a large team of employees from the department to come together and create a recommendation for the new structure. The process was formal, and my role was to facilitate the group through the process. From a change management perspective, involving employees in this significant decision has tremendous advantages, but as you can imagine, anytime you consider a restructure, the level of fear escalates.

One of the first steps is to get goals on the table—not only organizational goals but individual goals as well. Some of the company goals were to develop a structure that was more functional and efficient, better supported customer needs, addressed intradepartmental communication issues, and allowed the department to better utilize their people resources. We pushed the company further. Then they shared what they also sought was a structure that would save money and flatten the hierarchy. This was a critical goal and important to get on the table.

Now came the tough part. What were the individual's goals? Employees stated they sought a structure that would allow everyone to keep their jobs, allow people to better utilize their strengths, and provide more opportunities for growth, promotion, and enhanced teamwork. All this sounded great.

Then we pushed them further and had them get really honest. They shared that they didn't want to lose their status, they wanted to change as little as possible, they wanted their salaries to stay the same or improve, they desired administrative support, and they feared that individuals on the team would put their own interests above that of the group.

In this situation, the ability to assess all the goals was critical. At that point, the group could begin to put ground rules in place and establish boundaries with leadership in order to create safety for continued problem solving. Once the real goals were assessed, the group could determine which goals were worth maintaining and which needed to shift in order to best support the project efforts and respect individual needs.

Redefine Personal Meaning

In alignment with the notion of assessing and/or altering our goals, we can assist employees and ourselves in redefining personal meaning from the events we experience. Our reaction to events is ours to own (and change). Essentially, it reflects the ability to redefine or reframe our conversations in ways that empower us rather than strip us of our control.

If I am in conversation and someone raises their voice, I might assess that they are angry at me for my performance. In response, I might feel fear. In reality, it likely has nothing to do with me. If I reframe the issue (and perhaps my goal), I can see that maybe there is passion around the issue that is being displayed. When

I frame the event in that way, I can actually use their passion for improved problem solving.

Additionally, I often work with leaders who are afraid of conflict. They have employee issues they need to address and worry that having a difficult discussion with staff will negatively impact relationships. They are concerned that the conversation will hurt people's feelings or be more trouble than it's worth.

As an example, I worked with a leader who had an employee displaying behaviors with the team that were not productive. He would roll his eyes when she passed by, gossip with other employees, spread negative rumors, and never support change efforts. In conversation, she came to a very true realization. "I just don't like him, and because of that, I don't feel like it's worth my time to talk to him and address the issue. It seems easier just to let it go."

However, by not dealing with the situation, the rest of her team continued to be frustrated with this employee and eventually with her as a leader. They needed her to tackle this problem, and by not doing so her team's trust in her diminished.

As we discussed the notion of reframing, I asked her to consider another perspective. How could she frame the situation in a different way? What could a new goal be that would give her energy to address the situation? The way she redefined personal meaning was to say, "This is about the staff I care for. If I do not address this employee and his issues, I am harming them, and I care too much about them to do that." By reframing the issue, she provided herself with energy to move forward with this employee. Her emotional state changed, and she had the necessary conversation.

Here are some additional examples of common ways we define personal meaning and how we might shift and reframe to better support our needs.

Employee: When my leader doesn't acknowledge me, I think they are mad at me. I worry that I have done something wrong or they do not like me.

Redefine/Reframe: My leader is very busy, and I might need to proactively welcome her in the morning.

Employee: I am being taken advantage of by everyone around me.

Redefine/Reframe: I have a lot to offer, and people need my support. Perhaps I can consider some boundaries in order to protect my own sense of well being.

Employee: I made a comment in a meeting that I thought was brilliant, but no one said a word. They must think it was a dumb idea.

Redefine/Reframe: Perhaps it was a brilliant idea and people need time to process and digest it.

When we think about personal meaning, it links to the idea of assumptions. We make assumptions and create stories all the time. The key is to verify these assumptions in order to ensure we are placing the correct personal meaning onto our situations.

Strategy 3: Eliminate and Manage the Threats in Your Life

Fear always begins as a threat—threats to our safety and security, threats to our sense of belonging and affiliation, and threats to our self-esteem. Given the work you have done throughout this book, where do you experience threats in these three areas? Take a moment to summarize your learning about yourself.

_____

_____

_____

_____

As we seek to deal with fears in our life, we must manage the threats. Acknowledge your fears and discuss them. Talk about fears with friends, family, and those who you feel safe with. Get clear about what is threatening you, both real and perceived.

Avoid the Language of Fear

The language of fear drives the perception of threat. When we use the language of fear or engage in fear-based behaviors, we increase the level of threat between us and our employees. Understanding where you see fear-based behaviors or language playing out in your workplace is important. When we notice and become aware of these aspects of fear, we can begin to change them. Does your staff feel safe to speak up? Do they feel retaliated against in any way? (Even the subtlest ways can cause employees to withdraw.) Do they feel threatened? What areas are you exhibiting a language of fear in? Be aware of not only what employees say verbally, but also pay attention to their non-verbal cues.

Acknowledge Fear

As you get clear on your own fears, begin to create environments for your employees and team to engage in discussions about their fears. Help them to acknowledge their fears and create safety for them to do so. It is this lack of safety that leads to the feeling of threat and fear. Denial is a coping mechanism that can be helpful in some situations, but until you can bring fears to the surface, they cannot be dealt with. Without awareness, you will stay stuck in the emotion. When you stay stuck, you lose the ability to deal with the fear, and your outcomes will continue to suffer. When we can acknowledge fear and openly discuss and address it, we move people through the emotion and assist them in achieving a more productive emotional state, which in turn impacts our results.

Create Safe, Trusting Environments

Avoiding the language of fear also requires that we create safe, trusting environments. Creating safe environments requires attention to detail and listening. Ensure the physical space is non-threatening. We often have difficult conversations in offices where the boss sits behind a big desk and the employee across the table. This condition contributes to a sense of power and hierarchy and decreases safety for conversation. Another example is when the boss always sits at the head of a large conference table. It creates a power dynamic that affects people's ability to feel safe.

If we really want to engage in open communication, consider the language you use to frame the conversation. Be attentive to the environment you are setting up and ease threats in the physical setting. If you are having these discussions with your entire team, consider sitting in a circle or U shape. Monitor your body language so that people can speak more freely, and ask questions that engage them in conversation. Listen 90 percent of the time, and *never* retaliate for anything stated in a safe space.

Another tip for effectively allowing people to openly discuss their fears and concerns is to establish ground rules at the beginning of the meeting. Ground rules are conditions for conversation. They help to ensure that people engage in the conversation from an appropriate place. Common ground rules might be:

- Don't blame.
- Don't use hurtful words.
- Don't attack others.
- Speak honestly, but own your words.
- Be kind in your language.
- Speak for your and the group's higher good.
- Maintain confidentiality

As a leader, it can be your role to assist the group or individual in adhering to the ground rules. It can also be helpful to seek the assistance of a facilitator, particularly in environments where safety is not present or has been compromised in the past. The facilitator can serve as a non-biased voice to keep the group focused and keep the environment safe.

Acknowledging fear and discussing it can be a critical first step in helping yourself and others get clear on where they see fear and fear-based behaviors occurring. It can also be a first step in supporting increased awareness amongst your team members. Establishing environments of trust requires an ongoing commitment to the having conversations that keep people stuck. Continue to engage in these discussions. It is only through these conversations that we can assist ourselves and others in moving through the fear and conquering it.

Activity

In order to elicit people's fears, the following activity can provide a safe and somewhat anonymous way for individuals to get their fears on the table. There are a couple potential ways to conduct this activity depending on the level of group safety.

1. When safety is high, ask each individual to write their fears on post-it notes. One fear should be listed per note, so you will likely have five to ten (or more) post-it notes per person. Have them consider fears from the perspective of safety and security, affiliation, and self-esteem. Engage in an open discussion as each individual shares their fears.

2. When safety is low, you might have each person write their fears on a post-it note or slip of paper. Have everyone place their paper in a bucket. Mix them up and pass the bucket around the table. Have each person draw the papers out of the bucket until the bucket is empty. At this point, everyone will get slips of paper that others have written on. Then individuals can share the fears listed on the papers they drew. Since you have mixed them up, there is a sense of confidentiality, because employees are reading each other's fears and not their own.

Once you have clarity on the fears that exist in your organization or on your team, you can begin to influence them through the use of the additional strategies that follow. Without the ability for employees to be open and honest about their fears, the emotion stays hidden and impossible to address. We see it in our poor team results, but we continue to wonder why.

Minimize Negative Internal Competition

Often, organizations and teams create internal competition as a means of motivating employees to do better, improve, and excel. While this can be the result, high levels of competition within cultures can also foster behaviors that are self-promoting and destructive. Employees might put up barriers to others, sabotage efforts of teammates, withhold critical information, or tattle on each other in order to stay ahead. In highly competitive environments, employees spend time and energy trying to minimize the threats they are experiencing, and they do so at the expense of teamwork, outcomes, and collaboration.

Organizations should engage in more effective strategies, which might be to create effective team-based behaviors, establish a clear vision, and keep employees focused on rivalry with the real competitors. Be aware of the impact you might be creating with internal competition and reward systems. They might be having an unintended outcome.

As an example, I recently worked with an organization that had several restaurants within the same geographic market. The rewards system incentivizes individual facilities and inadvertently created competition between the seven entities in the market. Each restaurant manager had individual targets and was at risk of losing their jobs if they did not reach them. Instead of capturing customers and market share from their competitors, they began taking it from one another in order to reach targets. This can be an example of how fear and internal competition can play out when it is not managed correctly.

Strategy 4: Alter the Variables that Impact Appraisal

From our discussion of emotion, recall that the goals we seek and the appraisals we place on the situation drive our emotional experience. If we change our appraisals of the situation by altering the variables that generate that assessment, we can shift our emotional experiences from fear to something different (perhaps challenge or hope). The three areas we need to manage at this level are certainty, control, and blame.

When we evaluate the role of appraisal, we must recognize and appreciate the fact that individuals create stories and make assumptions around all the events that happen in our lives. We speculate why something is happening, and we hypothesize reasons people act in certain ways. When we don't know something or have gaps in our knowing, we unconsciously fill them in with our own story. How we describe our assumptions leads us down a path that is reflected in emotion. The problem surfaces when our story is incorrect and we spent time and energy on negative emotion based on appraisals of the event that were wrong.

When someone honks in traffic, do you assume they are honking at you or waving hello to a friend? Do you get angry, or do you wave and smile? When someone is late, do we assume they are lost and worry, or do we judge that they are always late and they will be here soon? When a coworker makes a comment in a meeting about our presentation, do we assume they are attacking us or bringing up a good point? We are always creating stories and making assumptions to fill in the blanks of our own knowing or trusting.

Leadership theorist Peter Senge also refers to these as mental models or deeply held assumptions[40]. As we develop these assumptions, it is important to recognize the impact they have on our behavior and emotional experience. When we assume someone is attacking us, we become angry and fearful. If we assume they are making a valid point, we are open and receptive—same event, different assumptions and appraisals, and very different emotions.

Part of our job, as leaders, is to recognize the minimizing assumptions that we and our employees make and fill in the gaps with truth. Our assumptions are driven from a variety of sources. Employees hold assumptions from past experiences in both their personal and professional lives. They create stories as they talk to other coworkers and can often find sources that help them justify their beliefs. Fear also leads us to create what are often very irrational assumptions about our behavior, the actions of others, and consequences.

Consider an employee who has previously been fired. Perhaps this employee has experience working in an organizational culture where fear was high and mistakes were opportunities to eliminate staff. Let's also assume that your team is very different. You are a leader who believes in a learning culture, and you promote the need to admit mistakes so that the team can learn and grow from these experiences. If this employee makes an error on your team, despite your best efforts for learning, they are likely to fall back on previous stories and assumptions. They might hide the error or blame others, fearing they will be punished. Their current story is that mistakes lead to being fired. Your role as a leader is to recognize the stories and assumptions your employees are making (along with your own) and help them to rewrite their assumptions given your leadership desires.

Here are some additional examples:

- If we think that physical exercise will positively impact our health, this story might impact how much we exercise.
- If we have a mental model that a great project idea won't be funded due to budget cuts, we limit our ability to consider broader options.
- If we believe that we are not capable of seeking a promotion within the company, we will not apply for the new job.
- If we believe that we are powerless, we fail to step out.

- If we think our company is going to make lay-offs, we might find another job (and you might lose great employees).

The stories we tell ourselves in all situations, and the assumptions we make, impact our decision making—they impact our appraisal of events, and it impacts our level of fear. When we can rewrite our stories and assumptions, it affects our judgment and appraisal of the situations we are in and can shift the entire emotional experience.

Here are common stories or assumptions we make when we are operating from fear.

- I have to put up with this because I could never find another job.
- It's a dog-cat-dog world, and I have no choice. I have to lead this way to get outcomes and fit into the company culture.
- If I don't do (blank), I will lose my job. (This could mean being available twenty-four/seven, not sharing your opinion, etc.)
- I'm not good enough for this promotion, so why bother?
- I never get credit for my work, and no one knows what I am capable of.
- At least I have a job, so I need to just put up with it.
- If I admit my mistake, I will be fired.

- My family just needs to understand. If I don't work, they can't enjoy all the privileges that they do.
- If I could just find time to exercise more, I would have more energy.
- I'm just going to come in and do my job. It's not like it matters anyway.
- I have no choice. I'm just stuck.
- I can't say anything. No one would listen anyway.
- I'm just a front-line leader. I have no voice in this company.
- If I work harder and longer, I will make more money and be happier.
- My job is my life. Without it, I don't know who I am.
- I am always being taken advantage of, and no one will support me.
- There are so many expectations. I am just confused. Just tell me what you want.
- That's not my job anyway, so why do I care?
- I have to protect myself, because no one else will.

These are just a few examples. Perhaps you can relate to them; and likely you have different ones as well. We all have stories, and we all make assumptions. There is no positive or negative. There is no judgment in it; it just is. The key is becoming aware of your own assumptions and the stories you tell yourself. They have one of the strongest impacts on your emotions, because they create your perceptions. As you review this list, which assumptions did you find yourself nodding yes to and feverishly agreeing? What assumptions or stories would you add to the list given your own experience?

Years ago, I was in a meeting with numerous individuals. I had what I perceived to be a bad experience with one individual. Based on his words and actions, I thought he was intentionally trying to diminish my credibility and make me look foolish. I was afraid that he would tarnish my image with others in the room. The stories were running rampant in my head. As I began to get clear on my assumptions, I found the strength to verify my stories—only to find that they were not true. His reactions, which I perceived as attacking and belittling, were actually his attempt to get clear on my role with the project. In all reality, the stories were my own—my own fears surfacing in my assumptions. I was feeling a lack of confidence with the senior leaders in the room and felt extremely vulnerable. While he owned his piece and how he approached the situation, I had a great deal of issues to work through as well.

As a different example, I had an experience where I was conducting a process improvement effort with a large group of leaders. As we began to action plan various opportunities and potential solutions, the group was putting up barrier after barrier.

"We've tried that before, and it didn't work."

"Leadership will never approve that."

"We don't have the budget."

"Employees don't have the time to do that."

The list went on and on.

In all reality, these barriers were based on assumptions which, at the time, were completely unsubstantiated. Often, our assumptions get the best of us. They can be like weeds that blossom and seed before we even have the chance to identify and pull them. When we alter the story, our emotional experience changes. When we change the underlying variable, we can shift the entire emotion. If we are deathly afraid of losing our jobs and tell ourselves that every action we take puts us at risk, we remain in fear—paralyzed and stuck. If we can get real about what is safe and what is a true risk, we alter our fear.

Below are also several statements that are cues that we are beginning to tell ourselves stories and make assumptions.

I should (insert behavior) because (insert reason).

What if…(insert negative outcome).

We can't because…(insert reason).

I wish I could…(insert desire), but (insert reason why you can't).

When you hear yourself using these phrases, be aware that you might be telling yourself a story. Get clear on what your story is and whether it is grounded in fear or truth. All too often, our negative stories and assumptions are based upon our fears and not centered in reality. When we say *should*, we are trying to justify something that is not in alignment with our underlying goal. When we begin down the "what if" path, we are making up scenarios and consequences for our actions that are likely not going to come to fruition. The word *can't* holds the same trap. We spend time and energy brainstorming all the reasons why not instead of exploring why something can work. Finally, "I wish" is a phrase that helps us get clear on our desires, but we often follow it with a defeated attitude. Pay attention to your "I wish" statements. They hold great clarity in terms of your goals. The place to be cautious is with the end of this phrase—the *but*. It holds our limiting beliefs and assumptions.

One final point of note: in seeking to manage our assumptions, we need to start by assuming good intent. All too often, our assumptions start and build because we are creating worst case scenarios and judging the intentions of others. We do this as a self-protecting mechanism when we are in a place of fear. We will judge ideas, judge people, and judge systems in an effort to protect our own needs. However, if we want to decrease our fear and that of others, we need to start by assuming positive intent and suspend our negative judgments. If we want to support a culture without fear, we must consider this relationship and work to minimize judgment.

Activity

In those situations where you are experiencing fear, what stories are you telling yourself? What assumptions are you making? Where do you hold judgments? Can you verify your assumptions with others to ensure your story is accurate? What is the truth behind your story? What would a new story sound like, and how can you create it?

Increase Individual Control

When we are in fear, we feel little control of our circumstances. We believe that others are responsible for our situations and that others control our destinies. This lack of control is a primary cause of our fear. This is an important point. Fear is about control, or rather, the perceived lack of control. The minute we assume control and ownership for our circumstances, the less we remain in fear; the second we take responsibility for our situation or aspects of our situation, the less fear we will experience. In reading this statement, consider accountability. Accountability is also about ownership. As we consider control and strategies that increase control, we can actually achieve a dual purpose—decreased fear and increased accountability. This is where we intersect the two concepts.

Therefore, our role as leaders is to help employees assume more control of their situations. We can do this in a number of ways, but perhaps the greatest strategy is to involve employees in changes and decisions that impact their work. In order to provide your employees more control, you as a leader must release control. In order to feel safe and trusting releasing control, you must assess why you are holding control to begin with. Are you controlling because you don't trust others? You don't trust yourself? Are you afraid of losing power or credibility? Why are you holding onto control? Only when we understand our own *why* can we effectively release it. It allows us to let go of the fear we have and open our hands to allowing others more control.

In order to decrease fear and increase individual control, we must embrace employee involvement in changes and decisions that affect them. We often hold the false assumption that leaders make the decisions and roll them out to staff; leaders make staff do what they are told. In reality, we experience greater success when staff is part of the change. They often have the best ideas for how to improve their work, and they are more bought into the solution when they get a voice.

If you have a change or solution that you need to make, consider involving employees at the very beginning of the process. Seek their input throughout the development of the project or change effort. Discuss boundaries in advance so employees know the guardrails they are operating within and let them guide the effort. If you have a change that you need to execute and employees were not given a voice in the development of a solution, allow for input and discussion. Share with them the items that are non-negotiable for the project, but also find ways that they can customize the effort to meet their needs. It is also critical that they understand the why. Instead of providing it to them, ask powerful questions to elicit the reasoning.

As an example, perhaps you need to find a more effective way to utilize staff resources within your department. At the beginning of the process, discuss the *why* with your employees. Have them brainstorm what is working and what is not within the current structure. They might say that the current leaders are highly competent, but the work is not aligned in a way to support the organizations strategy. Perhaps they feel like they need additional staff at the front line to support the needs of the department. Maybe they express a need for a shift in various types of staff. The conversation about what is working and not working can provide them a voice into the change.

If you already have a solution, help them understand why you are changing. Perhaps ask them to identify some of the challenges the department is experiencing and then present how the new change will address those challenges. The more they can come to the table with thoughts, actions, and ideas, the more likely your change is to be successful and the less likely they are to experience fear.

Many process-improvement methods have actually built in employee involvement as a mechanism for improved solutions and increased employee buy in. As you consider the solution to a given problem, we know that involving employees who know about the issue will generate the best results. It will also increase individual employee control and thereby decrease fear. The mere act of increasing acceptance automatically decreases the level of fear. When we implement strategies to increase acceptance, we organically lower fear.

Let's consider another example. You have a policy in your department that is not being followed. (Often I argue that organizations have too many policies, and that alone can lead to fear, but this is a different issue.) This particular policy is not up for debate. There is no changing it and no way to get around it. It is required that all employees follow the procedure for the safety of themselves and the organization. Only 50 percent of your staff is following the outlined procedure, and it is not consistent even with those 50 percent of employees. What would you do to ensure employees are following the policy? I posed this example to a group of leaders, and here were some of the common responses.

The number-one reason provided, above all others was, "Begin writing up and formally disciplining individuals who do not follow the policy." All too often we believe that accountability and punishment are synonymous. We think that holding others accountable to behavior and performance standards means we must establish and enforce consequences. This is far from the truth. Punishment does *not* equal accountability. Punishment leads to disempowerment, and disempowerment creates fear. Accountability is built from ownership. Help others own their choices. Consequences might follow, but you need to establish empowerment first.

The second reason given was, "Educate employees about the consequences of not following the policy." Again, we continue to think that we must instill fear through the establishment of punishment in order to achieve accountability.

Additional responses from the group begin to get us closer to effective mechanisms for establishing accountability. They stated, "Educate employees about the policy and what they need to do to be in compliance," or, "Explain why the policy is important for employees to follow." As we evaluate the additional responses, we are beginning to set the stage for helping employees to gain control and understand the *why*, not in response to fear, but as a result of a deeper purpose.

If the goal is to increase compliance, we must allow for the increase of individual control. Ideally, we would assist employees in understanding the importance of the policy. The best way to do this would be to allow them to come to that conclusion. Instead of feeding employees the reason for the policy, ask them to discuss it. Consider posing the question, We have a policy in place around (blank). Can we talk about the importance of this procedure? This allows employees to come to their own conclusions.

Add items from your perspectives that are not discussed. I would then recommend you share the data about compliance, indicating that less that 50 percent of employees are consistently adhering to the policy. At this point, open up the floor for discussion—not excuse making, but discussion. Consider stating, "It seems we are all in agreement that the policy is important, so I want to brainstorm ways that we can ensure 100 percent commitment to following the procedure." You might ask, "What gets in our way of following the policy, and how can we break down those barriers?" This allows you to hear employee's thoughts. More often than not, they will share valid reasons why something is not occurring. Once you eliminate those legitimate barriers, you not only impact compliance, but you have now increased commitment, given employees increased control, and decreased fear.

Leaders often argue that they don't have time for this type of discussion around every little change that they implement. While I agree that you have to select items worthy of discussion, I would also propose that the time you don't spend on the front end will absolutely cost you on the back end. What if you avoided the conversation and moved to discipline? The time cost of writing employees up, firing employees, and rehiring new staff far outweighs the time spent discussing the issue on the front end. In addition, these behaviors affect the rest of your team and have a negative impact on them as well.

There are many ways that we can involve individuals in our decision making and change efforts. The important point to remember is that by giving employees the perception of increased control over aspects of their job that impact them most, we decrease fear in our culture.

Activity

Below are two lists of questions. The first represents questions you might consider individually as you experience change. The responses to these questions will assist you in determining aspects of a decision where you can assume more control and accountability yourself. The second list reflects questions for you to consider as a leader when you are introducing change to your employees. Consider the following questions individually:

1. What aspects of the issue do I have control over?

2. Where can I let go of my previous beliefs surrounding this issue?
3. How significant of an issue is this for me? It is a deal breaker, or is it just a minor irritant?
4. Do I feel any personal defensiveness or offense around this issue?
5. What can I proactively do to assume more control? What might it look like for me to take more control and feel more empowered by the situation or issue?
6. How can I more proactively get information or contribute to the effort in a way that enhances my personal control?

Consider the following questions for changes and decisions that impact your team:

1. What is the problem, issue, decision, or change I am considering?
2. What impact will this issue have on my employees? Will it impact everyone or just certain groups/people? Is the impact significant or minor?
3. What control can I give employees in this decision?
4. What are the boundaries or non-negotiable items? What aspects of the change are required and not up for debate?
5. How can I structure a discussion with the correct individuals to seek input into the change?

Strategy 5: Decrease Uncertainty around the Unknown

Similar to issues of control, we know that high levels of uncertainty increase fear. This links to the discussion of assumptions in that we create elaborate stories when there is a great deal of uncertainty in our world. Where we don't have answers to our questions, we will generate them—right or wrong. In the face of uncertainty, we will seek to create equilibrium. This might occur through the creation of assumptions, gossiping with others, making up rules, or avoiding the issues.

As leaders, in order to decrease fear, we must increase certainty. We need to begin to stop telling ourselves stories and fill in the gaps for employees so the assumptions they believe are based in truth. A foundational strategy to decrease uncertainty is to establish clear expectations. We spoke of this in earlier chapters as we discussed the goal of accountability. When we establish clear expectations, we decrease the unknown, and employees can step into what's real for them and for you. Additionally, setting expectations is the basis of accountability. When managers provide little to no direction or they frequently change directions, employees are not clear on what leaders want from them, and they are unsure how to react and respond. In the face of this uncertainty, they assume they are not meeting expectations and become fearful.

A common leadership complaint is that employees are not doing what is required of them. They are not behaving as expected, they are not achieving individual and team objectives, and they are not following formal and informal protocols. The first question to pose to yourself is whether you have been clear on your expectations. We often think we have created clarity, but we leave our employees feeling helpless and unsure. They think they are doing what is required, but they never please their leader.

When considering expectations, we can define both quantitative goals and also agreements that we seek to maintain between our employees and us (or you and your own manager). When employees have clear expectations, they save time and effort focusing on things that are important. They have an in-depth understanding of where they should spend time and what is required of them in the work setting. In addition, they are able to contribute the best of themselves knowing these boundaries. The unknown is no longer a mystery, and when the unknown dissipates, fear is dispelled as well.

Activity

Consider the following questions as you determine expectations for yourself and others. Ask your employees if they can answer these questions.

- What do we want from employees in terms of performance?
- What do we need from them in terms of behavior?

- Where are individuals currently not meeting expectations, and how can I get clear in defining those aspects?
- What is most important to me in terms of work performance?
- Do my employees know the processes, policies, and procedures that are critical for our team?
- What is expected of you , as a leader, that others need to be aware of or that you should cascade to your team?

Be as Transparent as Possible

A second way that we as leaders can reduce the unknown is to be transparent in our communication and decision making. Remember that when information is lacking, employees will fill in the blanks with their own data; they will create their own stories. Transparency is about sharing necessary information with employees in a timely fashion. It centers upon giving people facts and data and being honest, particularly in situations where there is high intensity and risk of fear. It requires that we as leaders share not only the facts, but also reasons for decisions, intent behind our choices, and motives behind our evaluations. From a broad perspective, transparency refers to information flow within the organization and between key stakeholders. Remember, when we seek to create transparency, we want to develop a two-way flow of communication and information between our employees and us. Transparency is not only about them getting information from us, but also about employees safely sharing information up the chain of command.

The first recommendation when establishing transparency is to merely share information across the organization and your department. There are a number of reasons why leaders often miss the mark when it comes to simply sharing information. Sometimes we think we must hold messages and data in confidence, waiting for just the right time to release it. We want a formal communication plan and seek to ensure that everyone gets the message at the same time. Our intentions are grounded in the desire to ensure fairness and coordination of critical information across the organization. There are certainly circumstances where this approach holds significant value. However, I would challenge you to consider whether you could be more transparent with information or strategically release it at more frequent intervals as a way of decreasing the unknown and thereby decreasing fear.

As we consider this issue, what we need to be cautious of is the tendency to hoard information. Information is power, whether we intend for it to be or not. Be sure to effectively communicate, particularly during times of significant or rapid change, in order to prevent fear within your team. Being transparent supports trusting relationships, keeps others from creating their own stories around the issues, and enhances the effectiveness of change efforts, because people understand what is occurring and why.

Here are some additional thoughts in creating transparency and reducing the unknown:

- Don't be silent and don't encourage silence. Allow employees the time and space to discuss questions and concerns. Silence occurs when people are in fear and do not trust. Create safety for critical conversations. Solicit input from others.
- Be open and honest with information, opinions, and feedback and allow your employees to do the same. Don't lie to employees. If it is an issue you can't discuss, tell them so and provide them as much information as you can along with a timeline when more will be released. If you don't know the answer, say so and research it.
- Communicate well. Ensure timely, frequent communication and be consistent in your messages. Be sure you are telling everyone the same story and say what you need to say.
- Keep commitments that you make or renegotiate the commitment if you need to. We destroy trust and transparency when we don't follow through on our promises and commitments.
- Give people access to the information they need. Many companies use intranets or share point sites to ensure employees can locate data, reports, and facts that they need. Use these tools to support you.
- Admit your mistakes. When we are transparent about our faults, it creates a vulnerability that allows others to learn and feel trusting.
- Actively involve others in decision making. Ask for input, thoughts, and recommendations.

Transparency is a new buzzword and also a critical element to reducing fear. Of course, organizational leaders are always managing confidential information, but don't keep secrets when you don't have to. Following the tips above creates cultures of safety and trust that support us in navigating change efforts, achieving improvement, and obtaining results.

As you consider transparency, ask yourself the following questions:

- What am I not saying that I should be?
- What are the hidden rules in my organization that I need to challenge?
- Who needs to have this information? Are they getting it?
- Who absolutely cannot have the data, information, or facts?
- What data, facts, information, and messages do employees need in order to do their job well?
- What data, facts, information, and messages do your employees need in order to reduce their fears and anxiety?
- Is there safety for two-way conversation? Can employees share bad news or problems?

Have the Important, Difficult Conversations

It never ceases to amaze me how life continues to throw us situations that challenge us and shine light on the learning we need to encounter. As I write this section, I am working with a student who has been plagiarizing assignments. I normally take a learning approach to these situations, trying to manage them from the perspective of growth and development as opposed to punishment. I generally believe that people do not intentionally seek to make mistakes. However, with this particular student, I am struggling. He is not accepting responsibility; he's making excuses, which are ridiculous, and he has blatantly violated the plagiarism policy by cutting and pasting word for word a free online essay for multiple assignments.

What I am now keenly aware of is my own reaction and lack of tolerance. I am also contemplating the reaction this other student is assuming. It is the same situation we find ourselves in when dealing with employee behavior. I am frustrated by his behavior and lack of accountability. I feel I (and the school) have established very clear expectations around this issue, and my tolerance for his excuses, justification, and inability to accept responsibility is very low, if not nonexistent. What I am also very conscious of is the fear my student must be feeling. I am aware that his defensiveness and lack of accountability is truly a response to the sheer fear he must be experiencing. Not only is he at risk of failing my class, but he is at risk of getting permanently expelled from school.

This event is no different than what leaders experience every day with employees. We have the need to hold others accountable for performance and behavioral expectations, the desire to get work accomplished, and the yearning to build an effective team. My heart screams with compassion in one regard and also realizes that this behavior cannot be tolerated. How do we engage in difficult conversations around challenging issues that promote accountability and awareness? How do we help employees own their issues? How do we maintain empathy and caring and still give voice to the urgency and importance of the issue at hand?

We often have one of two reactions in these types of circumstances: avoidance or aggression. Below are some common reasons that interviewees stated for avoiding necessary conversations.

- "I am afraid that having the conversation will negatively impact my relationships."
- "I am so angry with my employee that I worry I can't control my own frustration."
- "I worry that people will be mad at me."
- "I don't have time at the moment to address it, and once I do, it feels like the issue is too old."
- "I am afraid my employees will retaliate."
- "I don't know what to say, and I feel like I can't hold my ground."
- "My employee is very manipulative/passive aggressive. When we start the discussion, they have good excuses or change the issue, and I lose control of the discussion. "
- It's too hard to pin them down.
- "There are political situations that often prevent me from addressing critical issues."
- "The issue doesn't seem that important at the time."

- "I can't deal with other people's anger and defensiveness very well."
- "I'm afraid of getting backed into a corner."

This shows how our fear in these situations actually gets in our way of effectively leading and managing critical issues. We make really good excuses in the moment to avoid such issues. Often, these excuses are based in our own fears. In reality, when we don't engage in the necessary discussion in a healthy way, we actually diminish trust and increase fear for both our employees and ourselves. What we need to recognize is that our conversations do not need to be either/or dialogues. It doesn't have to be a situation where we *either* have the discussion and make people mad *or* avoid the conversation and the issue continues. There is a way that we can have the conversation and maintain our employees self-esteem. We can address the issue and have our employees leave feeling supported by the discussion.

An opposite reaction that can occur when we are not having the right conversations is that we can go into a more aggressive mode. From this place, we allow our anger and frustration to take over, and we display hostile, destructive behaviors. Both of these reactions lead to an increase in fear.

When you seek to engage in difficult discussions, particularly around performance, consider the following tips:

- Think about the discussion and know your objectives in order to facilitate the most appropriate conversation. Every conversation looks different depending on the situation. Before you enter a discussion, be clear on what your goals are and what your ultimate intended outcome is for the discussion. If you are seeking a conversation of understanding and support, you will engage in the discussion from a much different perspective. Be clear on your boundaries and also know where you can flow in the discussion. Be cautious not to hold on too tightly to a given scenario and continue to allow for two-way dialogue.

- Take a coaching and a learning approach. All too frequently, we think we must enter these discussions from a firm, punitive perspective. After all, we want people to know we are serious. However, if you take a step back and come to the discussion from a learning perspective, you can lower the threat level, minimize defensiveness, and actually entertain a discussion about the issue in a way that both parties are heard. The second we allow defensiveness to crepe into the conversation, listening and learning get thrown out the window. Changing the approach you take from the very beginning can lead you down a very different path and can be much more effective in the long run.

- Listen, listen, and listen some more. As leaders, we make the mistake of thinking we must know everything. I encourage you to take a moment and just listen. Try to make 75 percent of your conversation about listening to the other individual. See how it shifts your discussions. Communication requires engaging in healthy two-way communication, which asks that you seek as much input from others as you are delivering. Remember that communication is not about talking. More importantly, it is about listening to help guide understanding.

- Ask powerful questions. In tandem with listening, we can achieve our objectives when we ask powerful questions. Set aside assumptions and pose a strong inquiry. This might be you stating an observation and then following up with a question. Perhaps say, "I noticed that when you are interacting with (name), you seem very defensive. Tell me a little about what you are feeling," or, "We've had discussions before about (fill in the blank). I am still seeing this behavior. What is going on for you in those circumstances?" Avoid using the word *why* in your discussions, as it can create defensiveness as employees seek to justify. Remember, when we are engaging in difficult conversations, we want to maintain openness, safety, and trust.

- Watch your non-verbal signals. Be aware and conscious of your body language and non-verbal signals such as tone of voice, facial expressions, and positioning of your body. Maintain an open environment for conversation. Additional powerful questions might be: "What do you see as the issue? What role do you think you played in the problem? How might you do it differently next time? What can we agree to in order to prevent this from happening in the future?"

- Seek to get all the necessary and relevant information on the table. It is common for us as individuals to make assumptions and decisions based on those assumptions before all the information is on the table. When we spend time sharing all the relevant information, it can either support our original hypothesis or change it. Either way, expanding the facts is critical to having important discussions.

- Provide balanced feedback. Too often, we only engage in conversations around performance problems. For leaders, it's actually the positive conversations that spark our energy. Be sure to provide balanced feedback as a way of positively reinforcing those behaviors that you want to see continue. Also, provide regular, timely feedback when you want to redirect performance. When we wait until the issue is critical, the conversation becomes more difficult. Manage issues as they surface and provide the feedback in the moment.

- Give honest, direct, compassionate feedback. Many managers struggle to be honest about employee performance. It is easy to tell someone when they are performing well but much more challenging to deliver a difficult message. Don't save it for performance reviews. Provide the information in a timely fashion and respond to their concerns as they surface. Also, consider face-to-face communication whenever possible. E-mail messages are often misconstrued, and telephone messages don't allow for you or your employee to pick up on subtle cues from non-verbal communication.

- Help employees own their issues. Accountability is about ownership. When we engage in the critical discussions effectively, we have the opportunity to help employees see their role in the issue. We can assist them in advancing their awareness and owning their part of the problem.
- Establish relationships. When we are in relationships of trust, it is easier to have the tough conversations. There is an established safety that promotes honest discussion. Develop relationships with critical stakeholders before you experience problems. It will make it easier when the road gets rough.

The tips above apply to a second type of situation as well. When employees are experiencing change, it is critical that we over communicate. Be sure that you apply to rules of transparency and engage in the discussion around fear during change.

Activity

When we consider difficult conversations, the first step is identifying what conversations need to be held. Often, if we are stuck or continuing to rehash an issue or event, there is a conversation behind it that needs to be held.

What issues do you find yourself continuing to discuss? Who do you frequently complain about?

When you go home at night, what conversations do you repeat with your significant other?

What is the conversation that you need to have?

What tips above would support you in engaging in that discussion?

Strategy 6: Change the Variables that Generate Threat

From our fear model, we explored briefly that threats and therefore fear can be minimized by experience, support, and confidence. As you begin to practice the strategies above, know that fear and threat is enhanced by three variables:

1. Lack of confidence in a given situation or in our experience to manage an issue, project, or circumstance.
2. Lack of support in helping us navigate new or difficult situations.
3. Lack of experience in a certain situations[41].

These three factors impact when and how fear surfaces. If you have a new project or a new job, you can lack experience, and the situation seems more fearful. All of the strategies above help to create environments where employees can gain confidence in their role and what is expected, as well as feel supported. When we have staff that are starting new assignments, performing new tasks, taking on new leadership roles, presenting in front of senior leaders, or assuming duties that they are not as comfortable with, it is important to remember that they will feel fear, anxiety, and worry. They will be concerned about messing up or making a mistake. They will worry about looking foolish or not competent. Their self-esteem is at risk, and they will feel threatened and fearful in that arena.

In order to address these significant fears, leaders can put support structures in place to increase employee confidence. All too often when leaders have problem employees, it is not the employee that is the issue, but rather the lack of support structures to assist them in feeling confident, competent, and supported. The tips below can assist you in building support structures to allow employees to function at their best:

- When you have new employees, put them with a buddy to support them the first couple weeks or months.
- If you have recently asked someone to assume new responsibilities, be sure to check in on them frequently. Do they have the right resources to be successful?
- Keep employees' personal feelings in tack through balanced feedback. Don't crush them with negative feedback before they even have a chance to build their confidence.

- Remember that when people feel pressured, they will move into fear. Continue to make sure that expectations are clear and support is provided. For employees, when there is perception that they are not meeting expectations, they will move into fear. Be sure they know the rules and how to play within them. Also, help them to understand when and how the rules can be broken.
- Recognize and reward performance that supports your vision. Don't always seek punishment.
- Give people experiences to establish success and decrease fear. Maybe they take on a stretch assignment before assuming a new role. Perhaps they assume a smaller project where they can be successful before jumping into the big pool.
- Understand people's previous experiences. Know that when others have had fear-based experiences, those emotions will translate into your environment until the trust has shifted.

As a leader, you need support and confidence as well. We are called to help others learn and grow, to help the organization succeed and perform, but we need support too. Be sure to address your needs and fill your bucket in a way that promotes your leadership strength.

- Find a champion or mentor to support you. Who is your champion? Finding a strong support person can mean the difference between success and failure, both personally and professionally. Consider finding a mentor or leadership coach either internal or external to your organization who can champion you beyond your circumstances—someone who can help you see other strategies and possibilities.

- Express your vulnerability. In some organizational cultures, it can difficult to admit mistakes, but for our own health and the health of our teams, it can be critical to show vulnerability. Saying things like, "This is the hardest things I've ever done," "I hate to admit this but…" can be challenging but important.

As final concepts in considering fear and issues of confidence, understand the role of power in your and others experience of fear in the workplace. Power surfaces in many ways from hierarchy and position power, to expertise and knowledge power. It can be knowing the right people, being articulate in challenging settings, having certain relationships, or exhibiting confidence. These power dynamics will impact the way we experience fear. When we are with and around people with power, we often move into fear more easily and frequently, even when the person does not intend to have that impact. We all have aspects of power. Where do you hold power over others (and may not even realize it), and how does it surface? Be aware of the power you hold and its impact on different individuals.

Finally, as we seek to manage fear in our workplaces, understand the role of time. Each of these topics and strategies could be a book in and of themselves. We all have different experiences and situations that generate fear for us. Be patient and appreciative of where you are and what fears are presenting themselves to you. Also, recognize that sometimes we move through fear quickly, and other times we can be seemingly stuck in it forever. As you learn to recognize and be aware of your fears, you will navigate them more quickly. As you begin implementing the strategies above, you will learn to make fear your friend and confidant.

CONCLUSION:
STIMULATING NEW GROWTH

As I left the room, fear permeated every ounce of my being. I could feel it in my body. My chest was tight; my stomach was in knots; and my legs were weak, feeling as if they could not support me. How would I process this event that had left me feeling so vulnerable? How would I make sense of what had just happened? How could I begin to get control of my situation and manage it from a place of strength and personal power? In this moment, I had a choice.

Would I remain lost and stuck in the fear that had washed over me like a giant wave, or would I surface from the water refreshed and renewed with growth and learning to bring forward? Despite my own fear, how would I lead others? How would I support them through this event? How could I lead from a place that left me feeling proud and true to me and my values? I answered these questions from the very core of my being. I found a place deep within myself that spoke my truth, and I acted from that space of knowing. I followed my own advice as I moved through my own experience of fear.

I invite you to take a moment of reflection and assess what gets in your way. What power and control do you have over your own decisions and situations, and how will use it? How do you want to lead?

In and of itself, fear is not a bad thing. In nature and in work, fear serves an important purpose. It offers us a sign when something might be amiss. It becomes the signal by which we recognize a potential threat. Listen to it, hear it, and act on it. Sometimes it will tell you to run—get out of your threatening situation. Sometimes it will tell you to fight. Perhaps it will communicate with you to wait. What we know, however, is that it always carries a message. When we can break down the causes and the true effects, it will support our action in a way that can catapult us forward. In the workplace, this signal is important and serves as a mechanism for strategic development, leadership development, and individual movement.

As we learn to assess the fear, navigate the fear, and respond in the presence of fear, we become more adapt as leaders, we position ourselves to guide others through the process, and we minimize the level of fear we create for others. As a leader, how will you guide others through their fear? How will you help them navigate the rough waters? How can you aid them in finding strength and truth?

FURTHER READING

Ashforth, B. E., & Humphrey, R. H. (1995). Emotion in the workplace: A reappraisal. Human Relations, 48(2), 97-125.

Ashkanasy, N. M. (2002). Studies of cognition and emotion in organizations: Attribution, affective events, emotional intelligence and perception of emotion. Australian Journal of Management, 27, 11-20.

Ashkanasy, N. M., Hartel, C. E. J., & Zerbe, W. J. (2000). Emotions in the workplace: Research, theory, and practice. In Ashkanasy, N. M., Hartel, C. E. J., Zerbe, W. J., (Eds.), Emotions in the Workplace. (pp. 3-18). Westport, CT: Quorum Books.

Ashkanasy, N. M., & Rush, S. (2004). Emotional rescue: A conversation with Neal M. Ashkanasy. Leadership in Action, 24(4), 15-18.

Basch, J., & Fisher, C.D. (2000). Affective events-emotions matrix: A classification of work events and associated emotions. In Ashkanasy, N.M., Hartel cEJ., and Zerbe, W. J., (Eds.), Emotions in the Workplace: Research, Theory and Practice. (pp. 36-48). Westport, CT: Quorum Books.

Beerel, A. C. (2003). How the power dynamics and the culture of fear in business organizations contribute to the gap between ethics and morality in business practice. (Doctoral dissertation, Boston University, 2003). Dissertation Abstracts International, 64(3). (UMI No. 3083821).

Cacioppo, J. T., & Gardner, W. L. (1999). Emotion. Annual Review of Psychology, 50, 191-214.

Cheng, C. (2007). A research study of Frederick Herzberg's Motivator-Hygiene Theory on continuing education participants in Taiwan. Journal of American Academy of Business, 12(1), 186-194.

Conklin, T. A. (2001). The call to nature: A phenomenological study of the experience of discovering and following one's calling. (Doctoral dissertation, Case Western Reserve University). Dissertation Abstracts International, (AAT 3027286).

Conklin, T. A. (2007). Method or madness: Phenomenology as a knowledge creator. Journal of Management Inquiry, 16(3), 275-287.

Creswell, J. W. (2007). Qualitative inquiry and research design (2nd ed.). Thousand Oaks, CA: Sage.

Daus, C. S., & Ashkanasy, N. M. (2005). The case for the ability-based model of emotional intelligence in organizational behavior. Journal of Organizational Behavior, 26, 4523-466.

Dillard, J. P., & Anderson, J. W. (2004). The role of fear in persuasion. Psychology and Marketing, 21(11), 909-926.

Dunn, S. C. (2001). Motivation by project and functional managers in matrix organizations. Engineering Management Journal, 13(2), 3-9.

Ellsworth, P. C. (1994). William James and emotion: Is a century of fame worth a century of misunderstanding? Psychological Review, 101(2), 222-229.

Ellsworth, P. C. (2003). Confusion, concentration, and other emotions of interest: Commentary on Rozin and Cohen (2003). Emotion, 3(1), 81-85.

Fay, E., & Riot, P. (2007). Phenomenological approaches to work, life and responsibility. Society and Business Review, 2(2), 145-152.

Fisher, C. D. (2000). Mood and emotions while working: Missing pieces of job satisfaction. Journal of Organizational Behavior, 21, 85-201.

Fisher, C. D. (2002). Real time affect at work: A neglected phenomenon in organizational behaviour. Australian Journal of Management, 27, 1-11.

Fisher, C. D., & Ashkanasy, N. M. (2000). The emerging role of emotions in the workplace. Journal of Organizational Behavior, 21, 123-129.

Folkman, S., Lazarus, R. S., Dunkel-Schetter, C., DeLongis, A., & Gruen, R. J. (1986). Dynamics of a stressful encounter: Cognitive appraisal, coping, and encounter outcomes. Journal of Personality and Social Psychology, 50(5), 992-1003.

Fredrickson, B. L. (2001). The role of positive emotions in positive psychology. American Psychologist, 56(3), 218-227.

Fredrickson, B. L. & Branigan, C. (2005). Positive emotions broaden the scope of attention and thought action repertoires. Cognition & Emotion, 19(3), 313-332.

Fredrickson, B.L., & Losada, M. F. (2005). Positive affect and the complex dynamics of human flourishing. American Psychologist, 60(7), 678-686.

Gittell, J. H. (2004, Winter). The power of relationships. MIT Sloan Management Review, 15-16.

Gordon Rouse, K. A. (2004). Beyond Maslow's hierarchy of needs: What do people strive for? Performance Improvement, 43(10), 27-31.

Grandjean, D. & Scherer, K. S. (2008). Unpacking the cognitive architecture of emotion processes. Emotion, 8(3), 341-351.

Humphrey, R. H. (2006). Promising research opportunities in emotions and coping with conflict. Journal of Managerial and Organization, 12(2), 179-186.

Humphrey, R. H., Pollack, J. M., & Hawver, T. (2008). Leading with emotional labor. Journal of Managerial Psychology, 23(2), 151-168.

Izard, C. E. (2002). Translating emotion theory and research into preventive interventions. Psychological Bulletin, 128(5), 796-824.

Lazarus, R. S. (1982, September). Thoughts on the relations between emotion and cognition. American Psychologist, 1019-1024.

Lazarus, R. S. (1991). Cognition and motivation in emotion. American Psychologist, 46(4), 352-367.

Lazarus, R. S. (1995). Emotions express a social relationship, but it is an individual mind that creates them. Psychology Inquiry, 6(3), 253-265.

Lerner, J. S., & Keltner, D. (2001). Fear, anger and risk. Journal of Personality and Social Psychology, 81(1), 146-159.

Marrs, P. C. (2007). The enactment of fear in conversations-gone-bad at work (Doctoral dissertation, Fielding University, 2007). Dissertation Abstracts International, 68(6). (UMI No. 3269179).

Maccoby, M. (2004, winter). Trust trumps love and fear. MIT Sloan Management Review, 14-15.

Manrique de Lara, P. Z. (2006). Fear in organizations: Does intimidation by formal punishment mediate the relationship between interactional justice and workplace internet deviance. Journal of Managerial Psychology, 21(6), 580-592.

Maxwell, J. A. (1996). Qualitative Research Design: An Interactive Approach. Thousand Oaks, CA: Sage.

Mills, J. V. (1999). Resistance to corporate changes: Perceptions of first-level supervisors and customer service employees (Doctoral dissertation, Walden University, 1999). Dissertation Abstracts International, 60 (06), (UMI No. 9931745).

Moustakas, C. (1994). Phenomenological Research Methods. Thousand Oaks, CA: Sage. Napper, R. (2009). Positive psychology and transactional analysis. Transactional Analysis Journal, 39(1), 61-72.

Nezlek, J. B., Vansteelandt, K., Mechelen, I. V., & Kuppens, P. (2008). Appraisal emotion relationships in daily life. Emotion, 8(1), 145-150.

Ollendick, T. H. (2005). Fears. *Encyclopedia of School Psychology*. Thousand Oaks, CA: Sage.

Pelletier, K. L., & Bligh, M. C. (2007). The aftermath of organizational corruption: Employee attributions and emotional reactions. Journal of Business Ethics, 80, 823-844.

Richardson, J. T. E. (1999). The concepts and methods of phenomenological research. Review of Educational Research, 69(1), 53-82.

Riggio, R. E., & Reichard, R. J. (2008). The emotional and social intelligences of Effective leadership: An emotional and social skill approach. Journal of Managerial Psychology, 23(2), 169-185.

Roseman, I. J., & Smith, C. A. (2001). Appraisal theory. In Scherer, K. R., Schorr, A., Johnstone, T.(Eds.), Appraisal Processes in Emotion (pp. 3-19). New York: Oxford University Press.

Russell, J. A. (2003). Core affect and the psychological construction of emotions. Psychology Review, 110(1), 145-172.

Ryan, M. J. (1996). Driving out fear. The Healthcare Forum Journal, 39(4), 29-32. Saengratwatchara, P. (2005). The threat of future downsizing and its ideological consequences (Doctoral dissertation, Southern Illinois University at Carbondale, 2005). Dissertation Abstracts International, 61(1). (UMI No. 3204671).

Sarros, J. C., Cooper, B. K., & Hartican, A. M. (2006). Leadership and Character, *Leadership & Organization Development Journal*, 27(8), 682.

Scherer, K. R. (1997). The role of culture in emotion-antecedent appraisal. Journal of Personality and Social Psychology, 73(5), 902-922.

Scherer, K. R. (2001). Appraisal considered as a process of multilevel sequential checking. In Scherer, K. R., Schorr, A., Johnstone, T. (Eds.), Appraisal Processes in Emotion (pp. 92-120). New York, NY: Oxford University Press.

Scherer, K. R. (2002). Introduction: Cognitive components of emotion. In Davidson, R. J. (Eds.), Handbook of Affective Sciences (pp. 563-571). Cary, NC: Oxford University Press.

Smith, E. R., Seger, C. R., & Mackie, D. M. (2007). Can emotions be truly group level? Evidence regarding four conceptual criteria. Journal of Personality and Social Psychology, 93(3), 431-446.

Stid, D., & Bradach, J. (2009). How visionary nonprofits leaders are learning to enhance management capabilities. Strategy and Leadership, 37(1), 35-40.

Stott, R. (2007). When head and heart do not agree: A theoretical and clinical analysis of Rational –Emotional Disassociation (RED) in cognitive therapy. Journal of Cognitive Psychology: An International Quarterly, 21(1), 37-50.

Sussan, A. P., (2006). Management by emotion (MBE). Competition Forum, 4(2), 433-437.

Sutton, R. I. (2009). How to be a good boss in a bad economy. Harvard Business Review, 87(6), 42-50.

Terez, T. (2001). When fear strikes the workplace. Workforce, 80(8), 24-25.

Thongsukmag, J. (2003). Fear in the workplace: The relationship among sex, self efficacy, and coping strategies. (Doctoral dissertation, Virginia Polytechnic Institute and State University, 2003). Dissertation Abstracts International, 64(6) (UMI No. 3095214).

Tiedens, L. Z. (2000). Powerful emotions: the vicious cycle of social status positions and emotions. In Ashkanasy, N.M., Hartel ceJ., and Zerbe, W. J., (Eds.), Emotions in the Workplace: Research, Theory and Practice. (pp. 36-48). Westport, CT: Quorum Books.

Wertlieb, D. L. (2004). Affective development. The Concise Corsini Encyclopedia of Psychology and Behavioral Science. Retrieved July 18, 2008 from *http://www.credoreference.com/entry/4410176*.

Whitworth, L., Kimsey-House, K., Kimsey-House, H., & Sandahl, P. (2007). Co-Active Coaching. Mountain-View, CA: Davies-Black Publishing. *http://www.netmba. com/mgmt/ob/motivation/herzberg/* retrieved September 8, 2011.

ENDNOTES

1   Folkman, S., & Lazarus, R. S. (1988). Coping as a mediator of emotion. *Journal of Personality and Social Psychology, 54*(3), 466-475.

2   Smith, C. A., & Ellsworth, P. C. (1985). Patterns of cognitive appraisal in emotion. *Journal of Personality and Social Psychology, 48*(4), 813-838.

3   Ashkanasy, N. M., Hartel, C. E. J., & Zerbe, W. J. (2000). Emotions in the workplace: Research, theory, and practice. In Ashkanasy, N. M., Hartel, C. E. J., Zerbe, W. J., (Eds.), *Emotions in the Workplace.* (pp. 3-18). Westport, CT: Quorum Books

4   Barbalet, J. (2006). Emotions. *Cambridge Dictionary of Sociology.* Chicago: Cambridge University Press.

5   Goleman, D. (1995). Emotional Intelligence. New York, NY: Bantam Books.

6   Barbalet, J. (2006). Emotions. *Cambridge Dictionary of Sociology.* Chicago: Cambridge University Press.

[7] Smith, C. A., Haynes, K. N., Lazarus, R. S., & Pope, L. K. (1993). In search of the "hot" cognitions: Attributions, appraisals and their relation to emotion. *Journal of Personality and Social Psychology, 65*(5), 916-929.

[8] Lazarus, R. S. (2006). Emotions and interpersonal relationships: Towards a person centered conceptualization of emotions and coping. *Journal of Personality, 74*(1), 9-46.

[9] Lewis, M. D. (2005). Bridging emotion theory and neurobiology through dynamic systems modeling. *Behavioral and Brain Sciences, 28,* 169-245.

[10] Izard, C. E. (1992). Basic emotions, relations among emotions, and emotion-cognition relations. *Psychological Review, 99*(3), 561-565.

[11] Schorr, A. (2001). Appraisal: The evolution of an idea. In Scherer, K. R., Schorr, A., Johnstone, T.(Eds.), *Appraisal Processes in Emotion* (pp. 20-33). New York: Oxford University Press.

[12] Roseman, I. J., Spindel, M. S., & Jose, P. E. (1990). Appraisals of emotion-eliciting Events: Testing a theory of discrete emotions. *Journal of Personality and SocialPsychology, 59*(5), 899 915. Scherer, K. R. (2001). Appraisal considered as a process of multilevel sequential checking. In Scherer, K. R., Schorr, A., Johnstone, T. (Eds.), *Appraisal Processes*

in Emotion (pp. 92-120). New York, NY: Oxford University Press. Smith, C. A., & Ellsworth, P. C. (1985). Patterns of cognitive appraisal in emotion. *Journal of Personality and Social Psychology, 48*(4), 813-838.

[13] Smith, C. A., & Ellsworth, P. C. (1985). Patterns of cognitive appraisal in emotion. *Journal of Personality and Social Psychology, 48*(4), 813-838.

[14] Smith, C. A., Haynes, K. N., Lazarus, R. S., & Pope, L. K. (1993). In search of the "hot" cognitions: Attributions, appraisals and their relation to emotion. *Journal of Personality and Social Psychology, 65*(5), 916-929.

[15] Izard, C. E. (1993). Four systems for emotion activation: cognitive and noncognitive processes. *Psychological Review, 100*(1), 68-90. Roseman, I. J., Wiest, C., & Swartz, T. S. (1994). Phenomenology, behaviors, and goals differentiate discrete emotions. *Journal of Personality and Social Psychology, 67*(2), 206-221. Scherer, K.R., & Ellring, H. (2007). Multimodal expression of emotion: Affect programsor componential appraisal patterns. *Emotion, 7*(1), 158-171.

[16] Schein, E. H. (1994). *Organizational Psychology (3rd ed.).* Upper Saddle River, N.J.: Prentice Hall Foundations of Modern Psychology Series.

17 Buckingham, M. & Coffman, C. (1999). First Break all the Rules. New York, NY: Simon and Schuster.

18 Cure, L. K. (2009). Fear within the workplace: A phenomenological investigation of the experience of female leaders. (Doctoral dissertation, Capella University, 2009). *Dissertation Abstracts International*, (UMI No. 3373458).

19 Eisenberger, R., Karagonlar, G., Stinglemanber, F., Neves, P., Becker, T. E., Gonzales- Morales, M.G., & Steiger-Mueller, M. (2010). Leader–Member Exchange and Affective Organizational Commitment: The Contribution of Supervisor's Organizational Embodiment. *Journal of Applied Psychology, 95(6)*. 1085-1103.

20 Izard, C. E. (1993). Four systems for emotion activation: cognitive and noncognitive processes. *Psychological Review, 100*(1), 68-90. Izard, C. E. (1992). Basic emotions, relations among emotions, and emotion-cognition relations. *Psychological Review, 99*(3), 561-565.

21 *defense mechanism.* (2008). In *The Columbia Encyclopedia*. Retrieved from http://lib.kaplan.edu/login?url=/login?qurl=http://www.credoreference.com.lib.kaplan.edu/entry/columency/defense_mechanism

22   *Dorland's   Illustrated   Medical   Dictionary*,   s.v.
      "displacement," accessed April 09, 2012, http://
      lib.kaplan.edu/login?url=/login?qurl=http://
      www.credoreference.com.lib.kaplan.edu/entry/
      ehsdorland/displacement

23   Lazarus, R.S. & Lazarus, B.N. (1994). Passion and
      Reason. Oxford University Press Inc. New York,
      NY

24   Sarnoff, I. (1962). Personality, dynamics and
      development. Hoboken, NJ, Wiley & Sons Inc.

25   Sarnoff, I. (1962). Personality, dynamics and
      development. Hoboken, NJ, Wiley & Sons Inc.

26   *Britannica   Concise   Encyclopedia*,   s.v.   *"defense
      mechanism,"* accessed April 09, 2012, http://
      lib.kaplan.edu/login?url=/login?qurl=http://
      www.credoreference.com.lib.kaplan.edu/entry/
      ebconcise/defense_mechanism

27   Cure, L. (2011-2011). Personal Interviews/
      Coaching.

28   Appelbaum, S. H., Bregman, M., & Moroz, P.
      (1998). Fear as a strategy: Effects and impact within
      the organization. *Journal of European Industrial
      Training, 22*(3), 113-139. Maccoby, M. (1991).
      Closing the motivation gap. *Research Technology
      Management, 34*(1), 50-51. Suarez, G. G., . (1994).

Managing fear in the workplace. *The Journal for Quality and Participation, 17*(7), 24-31.

[29] Briksin, A. (1996). Fear and learning in the workplace. *The Journal of Quality and Participation, 19*(7), 28-34.

[30] Bowey, A. (2005, Winter). Motivation: The Art of Putting Theory into Practice. European Business Forum, (20), 17-20.

[31] Witte, K. & Allen, M. (2000). A Meta-Analysis of Fear Appeals: Implications for Effective Public Health Campaigns. *Health Education and Behavior*, 27(5), **591-615.** Williams, K. C. (2011, Oct.). *Improving fear appeal ethics. Journal of Academic & Business Ethics*, (5), 1-24.

[32] Nielsen, J., Shapiro, S. (2009). *Coping with fear through suppression and avoidance of threatening information. Journal of Experimental Psychology: Applied*, 15(3), 258-274.

[33] Tugade, M. M. & Fredrickson, B. L. (2001). Resilient Individuals Use Positive Emotions to Bounce Back From Negative Emotional Experiences. Journal of Personality and Social Psychology, 86(2), 320-333.

[34] Cure, L. K. (2009). Fear within the workplace: A phenomenological investigation of the experience of female leaders. (Doctoral dissertation, Capella

University,2009).*Dissertation Abstracts International,* (UMI No. 3373458).

[35] Goetz, J. L., Keltner, D., Simon-Thomas, E. (2010). *Compassion: An evolutionary analysis and empirical review. Psychological Bulletin* ,136(3), 351-374

[36] Bohnke, J. M. (2000). An analysis of cognitive discrepancies regarding supervisors' use of fear as a management tool in the workplace. (Doctoral dissertation, University of La Verne, 2000). *Dissertation Abstracts International, 62(2).* (UMI No. 3004765)

[37] Kersten, J. M. (2007). Emotions in employee-supervisor workplace relationships: The lived experience of women professionals (Doctoral dissertation, University of St. Thomas, 2007). *Dissertation Abstracts International, 68*(3). (UMI No. 3255585)

[38] Cure, L. K. (2009). Fear within the workplace: A phenomenological investigation of the experience of female leaders. (Doctoral dissertation, Capella University,2009).*Dissertation Abstracts International,* (UMI No. 3373458).

[39] Izard, C. E. (1993). Four systems for emotion activation: cognitive and noncognitive processes. *Psychological Review, 100*(1), 68-90.

[40] Senge, P. (2006). The Fifth Disciple: The Art and Practice of the Learning Organization. DoubleDay: New York, NY.

[41] Cure, L. K. (2009). Fear within the workplace: A phenomenological investigation of the experience of female leaders. (Doctoral dissertation, Capella University, 2009). *Dissertation Abstracts International*, (UMI No. 3373458).